HOPE IN 'BOMB CITY'

HOPE IN 'BOMB CITY'

Ben Forde
with Chris Spencer

Lakeland

MARSHALL, MORGAN & SCOTT

Lakeland
Marshall, Morgan & Scott
a Pentos company
1 Bath Street, London EC1V 9LB

ISBN 0 551 00824 5

Verses at chapter heads are by the following:
Sir John Arkwright, chapter 11
Horatius Bonar, chapter 12
Len Magee, chapter 4
W. Elmo Mercer, chapter 10
John W. Peterson, chapters 1, 3, 6
Esther Kerr Rusthoi, chapter 7
Marijohn Wilkin, chapters 2, 5, 8, 9

Printed in Great Britain by
Hunt Barnard Printing Ltd., Aylesbury, Bucks.

9790M 01

DEDICATION

Dedicated to
Lily, Keri and Clive
and the wives and children of all my colleagues
without whom our lot would be tougher still

It is my prayer that this personal
story will be used of God to help
establish in the heart of the reader
a lasting peace, and that such peace
will be instrumental in helping to
build that broader peace for which
our nation cries out.

BEN FORDE

Acknowledgements

The authors wish to thank the many friends who have encouraged them with their enthusiasm for this project and who have supported them from the beginning in believing prayer. Thanks also to Avril Cummings and Jennifer Fraser for typing the manuscript with speed, expertise and care; to Lily and Jan for making valued constructive criticism; and to Dan Wooding, who suggested the title.

For obvious reasons the names of some of the characters in this book have been changed. The names of all central characters are actual.

Contents

Some of the more significant Scripture verses quoted in this book will be found as follows:

1

Eight feet from death

He knows each turn of the pathway,
He is a light for my feet,
He has the power to keep me,
Tho' many dangers I meet.

Belfast – 'Bomb City' – was enjoying a respite. There had been no explosion, not even a bomb scare, for almost two days. What was more, the weather was on our side. The morning's gathering of rain-filled clouds had been chased off by a spring breeze, ushering in warm, soft sunshine that bounced off the smooth pavements and wrapped the city in good spirits. The streets buzzed contentedly with the comings and goings of shoppers and city workers, while over in Botanic Gardens office girls on wooden benches giggled and nibbled at sandwiches while old men leaned on knobbly sticks and wondered where the years had gone.

It was a good day for reflection. A good day to remember the peaceful times. Before, on a pleasant afternoon such as this, the city would sigh under the gentle touch of summer and relax awhile. On this day too the sunshine teased and tempted, but Belfast could not be fooled; the sun-brightened colours of spring were not the true hues of this sad city: she lived under cloud. And although once as bright as a beautiful girl with sparkling eyes, now, despite the cosmetic efforts of the sunshine, she was a widow in black with scars on her face. You had only to look around at the city centre or out to the Falls Road, the Shankill Road, or one of her many other battered limbs, to know the grim truth of that. But on this afternoon, glorious rays of sun pouring into her lap, the city of Belfast could be forgiven for dreaming. For dreams don't last long. This one soon would turn to nightmare.

A man was running down the street, waving his arms and shouting. I was about to step on to the zebra crossing, but spun round and recognised Constable Lloyd Allen, a recently recruited uniformed colleague. His cry was one which, at that time, we seemed to be hearing almost every day – but it was no less alarming for that.

'A bomb!' he was calling. 'There's a bomb in Botanic Avenue!'

He saw me and raced up, his face flushed with the deadly urgency of his mission. The warning had come through on the telephone, and while other men were quickly being detailed, Lloyd had come on ahead to warn the shoppers. Moments later we were both sprinting through the laughing sunshine on our way once more to act out the well-rehearsed pattern of this lethal hide-and-seek. The routine was now as natural as breathing, but that didn't dull the quiet terror which rose like a black monster at the back of your mind. It made your heart pound and dragged the moisture from your throat. It screwed up your nerve-ends and murdered your smile. And, when it was all over, it spat you out between its razor teeth and left you sweating and limp. Unless the bomb got you.

As we hared into Botanic Avenue, both of us shouting the warning now, we split up, Lloyd taking one side of the street and I the other. We ran into shops and along the crowded pavements, old ladies and young mums with kids scooting out of our way, not in blind panic, for that can be as explosive and as fatal as any bomb, but in an unspoken drill in which folk hurriedly but calmly worked with one another to clear the area. The shopkeepers had it worst. They had the job of searching their premises and perhaps the horror of finding a packet of gelignite rubbing shoulders with the table salt and baked beans. On this occasion it was quickly established that the bomb – if there *was* a bomb; occasionally the warning telephone call would be a hoax – was not in the shops.

Lloyd and I were now searching vehicles parked in the street, and other uniformed officers who had joined us were redirecting traffic and aiding the shoppers' exodus. We went from one end of Botanic Avenue to the other, all the time not knowing where or when the explosion would come – or what would trigger it. If it was rigged to a timing device then of course it would happen at the precise moment chosen, probably at random, by the misguided person who had made it. If it was linked to some sort of action – like the lifting of a car boot or the turn of an ignition key – then it could be hours before the explosives were detonated. Unless, of course, it could be discovered and defused, but the number of terrorist bombs thus rendered harmless are few compared with those which succeed in their dirty work.

What of this bomb? We had completed the usual

thorough search but no trace of it had been found. What now? Was it a hoax after all?

Posnett Street leads off Botanic Avenue and on the corner of the two I met up with Lloyd Allen again. We quickly went through the possibilities. Should we make a personal search of the shops? Get the owners of the cars and vans to open up their boots and bonnets? Was there somewhere we hadn't looked?

As we talked I leaned against a green van parked just in Posnett Street. Lloyd stood in front of me, casually looking along the side of this vehicle. Suddenly he broke off in mid sentence and pointed towards the passenger door.

'The window's open,' he said evenly.

When you're looking for explosives you become almost fanatically suspicious of the simplest irregularity.

He poked his head in through the open window and withdrew it a few seconds later.

'There's a funny smell in there. Could you check it?'

I gently opened the van door, looked and smelt inside, and knew at once that sense of danger that rattles your nerves and shoves a lump like a rock up your throat. But that's not enough. Instinct is a great ally, but suspicions need to be confirmed. The smell was the bitter-sweet smell – like marzipan – that's given off by gelignite, but I needed some sort of *proof* that there was cause for alarm. The lead had to be followed up. Humanly speaking, to hang around that van for a second longer was folly. But if this was where the bomb lay hidden it was my duty to find out. If *I* didn't do it someone else would have to.

It's at moments like this that suddenly a man realises how much he loves life; how much his family and friends

12

mean to him. But there's a job to be done, so he fights back the fears and gets on with it, praying to God that he'll still be around tonight to tuck the kids into bed . . .

In the back of the van was a blue and yellow tarpaulin – something like a tent. Slowly, ever so slowly, I lifted it and the last dab of moisture vanished from my throat. Underneath were two brown paper parcels. One was about fourteen inches by twelve and appeared to be torn open at the end. Inside I could see a grey, granulated substance. The other was bigger, about eighteen by ten, and had bits of material and paper sticking out of it.

It's a curious fact that the terrorist campaign in Northern Ireland is being fought in part under the guise of innocence. Two men call at a house where a woman and her little girl are the only ones home. The men say they have come about car repairs and the woman invites them in to watch television while they wait for her husband to return. When he arrives, one of the men pulls out a revolver and commits bloody murder on the living room carpet. In the same way, a couple of parcels in the back of a van could be harmless goods awaiting delivery. They turn out to be powerful bombs which, if undetected, could kill or maim any number of passers-by. This says much about the type of people which the RUC (Royal Ulster Constabulary), the UDR (Ulster Defence Regiment), and Her Majesty's Forces are dealing with in this part of the UK. They are the type of people who find some sort of sick pleasure in telling you there's a bomb in Botanic Avenue, knowing that the security forces will rush around on a fruitless, frustrating search because the bomb is in Posnett Street, just round the corner. But today, almost by chance, we'd tumbled them.

13

I got out of that van a lot faster than I got in. I'd seen enough to know that this was the bomb, and once again Lloyd and I were running down the street, but this time making our escape as we shouted the warning. Shoppers tumbled from the little grocer's only a few yards from the van, and I rushed into another shop to raise the alarm. As I came out the only thought in my head was to get as far away from that vehicle as possible. But you can't stop being a policeman and I halted as I saw two old ladies walking down Botanic Avenue towards the corner of Posnett Street. I don't know how they got there – the street had been cordoned off – but the fact was they were innocently heading towards the van. Without thinking, I dashed across the road, past the van, and quickly turned these ladies round and set them hobbling off in the direction from which they had come.

Back in Posnett Street Lloyd and I were faced with another problem. Believing the bomb to be in Botanic Avenue that was the only street to be cordoned off. As yet we hadn't had time to close Posnett Street and now traffic was coming along towards the van. Quickly we stepped in and gestured to the drivers to stop and go back. More officers were now arriving to help control the situation, but there's always the unexpected: from somewhere came a concrete-mixer lorry. I was standing opposite the green van when the lorry passed in front of me – and it was at that precise moment that the van was shattered into a million pieces, and the houses shook and groaned. I don't remember much about it, apart from the first ear-splitting crash and the invisible sheet of force which kicked my legs from under me. I suppose I was about eight feet from the van when it went up. What

14

I didn't know at the time was that if the lorry hadn't been between us I would have become the latest fatality on the RUC's list of members killed in the line of duty. I've become rather fond of concrete-mixer lorries since then!

As I struggled back into consciousness I saw the blurred outline of a young woman. She was tugging at my tie and loosening my collar and asking me if I was all right. I was, apart from pains in my head and back and a pounding in my ears. Others hadn't been so fortunate. The driver of the lorry had lost part of his arm – he'd had it outside the window at the time of the blast – and other folk, including Lloyd, suffered broken limbs. Thank God, there hadn't been any fatal casualties.

Before long the emergency services were pouring into the area and I was being treated for minor injuries, lying out on the warm pavement and staring up at a circle of unknown faces. After a while I was able to sit up and soon I found myself being helped into a car and driven by a fellow officer to Belfast City Hospital. I remember reciting to him the words of a hymn which came to me as my mind adjusted to the events of that lunchtime:

> O love that wilt not let me go
> I rest my weary soul in Thee;
> I give Thee back the life I owe
> That in Thine ocean depths its flow
> May richer, fuller be.

I believe he thought I was still suffering from the shock of the explosion, which I was, physically; but mentally I was aware of a deep, steady peace which I knew came from outside my own resources. This peace, I recall, struck me because as my mind cleared I began to realise just how close I had come to death, and how very sure I felt that, even if the worst had happened, I would have had absolutely nothing to fear. Everything was all right. That's an assurance that can be tested only when you look death in the eye. When it happens, and your faith stands firm, you feel pretty good inside.

At the hospital they treated me for shock and spent half an hour picking fragments of glass out of my hair. When I asked, they told me my wife had been informed that I was all right.

This happened on Tuesday 9th April, 1974.

That year the RUC dealt with 1007 bombs; 291 of my fellow officers were injured; 13 lost their lives.

2

Beginnings

The faintest flicker of faith, my friend,
   is all He needs to see;
There's no need for words when your
   thoughts are heard,
He'll find you like He found me.

When I was a boy – all grazed knees and scuffed shoes –
I used to kick an old football against the fence that
fronted the little patch of grass we called the front garden.
Once, I belted that ball so hard it broke two of the stakes
and my Dad caught me and made sure I would never do
the same again – and he did it simply by his tone of voice
and his expression; never did he so much as raise his
hand against me. That was fortunate for me because he
was a big man and had he chosen to use corporal punishment I would have known all about it. He had a good
right hand did my Dad. He was a butcher, and you need
a strong arm to slam a meat-cleaver through solid bone.
But he was never rough. In fact, as Dads go, he was
quite gentle; he smiled quickly and often and had a warm,
cheerful nature.

His hobby was greyhounds. He always had two or
three around the place and he kept them in a couple of
dog-sheds in the back-yard. No dogs ever ate better,

thanks to the scraps Dad brought home from work, and no sheds were better maintained; the straw was always fresh and the floors ever spotless.

Those dogs gave Dad enormous pleasure, and as I think back I realise that the leads which hung on the back of the scullery door, along with Dad's old cap and bicycle clips, just about summed up his worldly possessions. But whatever he lacked in the riches of this world, he was far from poor in terms of contentment, fulfilment, satisfaction – commodities which, in this affluent age, seem elusive to many, despite their comparative wealth. Or perhaps because of it.

The highlight of Dad's week was Saturday night when he would slip the leads on to the greyhounds and take them to the stadium in Dungannon where he would race them for the sheer thrill of watching the dogs whip round the track, forever pursuing the unobtainable hare.

My mother could not share Dad's Saturday night delight, except perhaps from a distance, for she suffered badly with rheumatoid arthritis and for years spent much of each day in a chair in a corner of the front room while her kids grew up around her and her husband went to and fro on his business and back and forth with his dogs.

I believe it distressed Mum that she couldn't get about to give my sister Leah and me the treats which mean so much to children, but I don't think we ever missed out for there was always Aunt Sarah, Mum's sister. Aunt Sarah lived with my grandmother in a house in Redcar Street, Belfast. Having no children of her own, and being acutely aware of Mum's disability, she looked upon us as her own family and took pleasure in spoiling us at the slightest excuse. She would come to our house once a week, regular as clockwork, and she never came empty-handed. I can see her now, turning the corner into our street, a bulging shopping bag in each hand and a wide smile on her face as Leah and I sprang through the front gate and raced along the smooth pavement to greet her. And all the way back to the house we would skip along, laughing and grinning and trying to peek into the bags.

Once indoors, out would come all sorts of delicious wonders: cream cakes, strawberry jam, home-made pies and tarts – all the magical, mouth-watering delights which would turn tea-time into a rich feast of edible dreams.

Sometimes, when Mum had to go into hospital, we would stay with Aunt Sarah and allow her (though we didn't take much persuading) to shower us with all the enjoyments she could muster. And come holiday time, it was Aunt Sarah who took us to build sand-castles and swallow ice-cream on the golden shores of Portrush.

We have much to thank Aunt Sarah for. She was everything Mum couldn't be. Perhaps without her, two children would have missed out on the sheer pleasure without which no childhood is complete.

But Mum gave to us in other ways, equally as important though perhaps not so much fun, and I do not believe that her years of inactivity were wasted. Mum had a deep, strong faith and many a time I would burst through the front door to find her praying or delving into her battered old Bible. She was a real saint. Not a pious, larger-than-life, stained-glass window Saint. But a simple, quiet and loving saint who prayed for Leah and me and taught us by both instruction and eloquent example the principles of Christ's teaching. She possessed

19

a wisdom born out of travelling the hard road of suffering and shared with us the practical, down-to-earth lessons she had learned along the way. She was a good tutor in the subject of life, as was Dad, and children growing up in the sometimes strained atmosphere of life in Northern Ireland needed to be taught aright.

A word which cropped up now and again was 'sectarianism' – a nasty, spiky word. We didn't know the meaning of it when we were kids, but we knew what it was: we were always conscious of a 'them and us' situation. Our family was Protestant and we lived in a predominantly Protestant street – Craigwell Avenue, Portadown. Things were never so bad that there was any real hostility between the two groups, but we had separate schools with different school colours, and as a result some of the children from each school tended to gang together. Occasionally one gang would pick a fight with another, but this was usually the result of youthful rivalry; it had little to do with Protestants and Catholics; the banners under which they rallied might just as easily have borne the names of other, less bitter, traditional opponents.

The segregation was real enough, though, and there were always those kids who would take the religious divide as an opportunity to go around bashing or humiliating those on the other side. For this reason I always took the long, 'safe' route home, rather than cutting across through a Catholic area. But sometimes it wasn't possible to avoid entering the other group's territory, such as when we were on an important expedition, like a visit to the local cinema. That meant running the gauntlet and more than once I got caught.

On one occasion when Leah and I were heading for the picture-house, a group of Catholic boys stopped us and made us hand over our money. I got my own back, though. A couple of weeks later I came across the leader of this gang on his own and gave him a good hiding. But I don't think I ever thought of Catholics as natural enemies; only certain individuals were regarded as such, and those included bully-boy Protestants.

This attitude prevailed in my mind because it prevailed in the home. There, Mum and Dad taught us to mix; and our home, for all the scrimping and saving necessary for a working-class household in the 1940s, was rich in the things that produce a healthy, balanced mind. Ever since I can remember, Leah and I were taught that all men are equal and that their religion and politics are their own business and to be respected.

'No man is bad because of a label,' Dad would say, teaching us tolerance. It didn't always sink in, of course, but it began to make sense to me when Mum started to get really bad and Dad's boss, a round-faced, jovial man with a loud laugh, came round with his wife and a bunch of flowers one Sunday afternoon. They came almost every week after that and always brought a little gift with them. They were Catholics.

Nowadays I don't talk much about Protestants or Catholics, except when I have to use such labels in the course of my work. In God's eyes there are only two classes of human beings: those who love him and those who don't. Those who love him are called Christians, because they are seeking to follow the example of Christ. When I was sixteen I came to realise that I wasn't doing this; that I wasn't a Christian. This disturbing truth, with all its unhappy consequences of God's judgment on the sinful, unrepentant heart, was opened up for me, like a flower in the sun, and laid bare for my uncomfortable inspection one Tuesday evening during a gospel mission. I had been invited to attend by some Christian friends. Not that this was the first meeting of its kind I'd been to – I had attended various squashes, barbecues, tent missions – but the gospel had always failed to move me. On this night, though, it was different. For some reason – which I can only attribute to the working of the Holy Spirit in my heart – the message was getting through. Christ's death on the cross, in which he suffered for the sins of the world, wasn't simply a universal, all-embracing act of love and sacrifice; it was also a personal transaction, in which he had offered himself in Ben Forde's place. Forgiveness and salvation were there, complete and waiting for Ben Forde to take them. All Ben Forde had to do was repent of his sins (an old-fashioned, unpopular word, but without equal), turn his back on his old, self-sufficient life, accept God's forgiveness through Christ, and begin living for him in the strength and enabling of the Holy Spirit.

Now it was all clear to me. And somehow I sensed God was calling me to make that commitment.

But that night I turned down God's offer and went home to bed.

You can't escape God, though. His Holy Spirit is more persistent in pursuing his subject than any detective ever was. Occasionally, when someone he is calling continually rejects his loving approach, he may withdraw. That is a black day for any person whom God is seeking to reconcile to himself, for there is no guarantee that the Spirit will ever call again. And it is impossible to find God without the Spirit as guide. Thank God he doesn't give up on many reluctant disciples.

I don't think I would have called *myself* reluctant on that night in August, 1957; perhaps I was just a slow starter. I knew that God had spoken to me and that I had to surrender my life to him, but perhaps I felt I needed a few more answers before I could hang the 'Under New Management' sign on my heart. Evidently God didn't agree, because in the four months which passed before I finally yielded I don't think I learned anything new. There were plenty of lessons to learn and mysteries to behold *after* my conversion, of course, but that was yet to come.

On Christmas Eve I joined in the festive celebrations at the printers where I worked – I joined when I was fourteen as a tea/delivery boy – and I suppose I had my share of eating, drinking and being merry, along with many other folk from the works. But it's a curious and wonderful fact that, no matter how loud and stirring the noises coming in your ears, the Holy Spirit's whisper in your heart is always louder and more moving. Next morning – Christmas morning – I was more aware than ever that God was calling me, and as I set out for Drumcree Parish Church, where I worshipped every week, it was with a sense of repentance and a desire to own the peace of God in my soul.

There was no dynamic sermon, no hammering of the Bible, no emotional appeal. But the hungry man doesn't need his food swept in with a fanfare on a silver platter: he simply needs to be led to the table. On this morning

God met me at his communion table as his food for the soul came to me through the words: 'You that do truly and earnestly repent of your sins . . . draw near with faith.'

That was all I needed – a confirmation of God's invitation. I didn't need a further explanation of Christ's sacrificial death and of the response he expected from me. Since August I had thought long and hard about these things. Now God, I believe, was stretching out his hand to me, coming to meet me as I took those all-important first steps towards him.

In my heart I responded with words which, over the years, must have been uttered by many hundreds of Christian pilgrims as they have set out on their journey to their heavenly home:

> Come into my heart, Lord Jesus.
> Come in today, come in to stay,
> Come into my heart, Lord Jesus.

That Christmas was a white one – or, to be more precise, a dirty-grey one, the crisp snow having turned to slush in the streets – and on my way to the church that morning I had picked a route along the pavements and dodged beneath the dripping trees, my heart heavy with the need to get my relationship with the Almighty straightened out. The walk back to the house was very different; the confidence of sins forgiven and the inspiring prospect of a new life in Christ lifted the burden from my soul and in its place I felt the deep and profound peace of God.

I don't recall the physical aspect of that brief journey. I suppose I sploshed my way through the slush. But inwardly my feet didn't even touch the ground.

There was no flash of light from heaven that morning. Craigwell Avenue did not become a Damascus Road. I knew nothing of the awesome breakthrough which God made into the life of Saul. But just as surely as the persecutor of Christians became a changed man that day, so on this Christmas morning, Ben Forde, printer's apprentice, received new life from the Lord.

This doesn't mean that I'm something special. It simply means that God deals with us individually, and that his grace to one is no less than his grace to another. And it means he can fully satisfy the need of the human heart. But he feeds only the hungry.

Fall in for adventure

Hold my hand while travelling through this land,
Hold me with your precious, nail-pierced hand;
Lead me on the tangled, winding way,
Lead me on and never let me stray.

It was a cold, clear February morning when our street was bathed in pale sunlight and the frost sparkled on the pavements and cracked under your shoes. I stood at the gate and watched with the silent houses as Dad steered his old bike around the ice patches and blew little clouds of steam into the sharp air. Before he reached the corner he turned his head and called out in soft, scarf-muffled tones:

"'Bye, son. See you.'

I raised my hand and smiled, fond memories chasing through my mind and the faintest glimmer of an ache calling out from somewhere deep within.

His bell rang sweetly, he looked this way and that, and then that old bike rattled him round the corner and out of sight.

Indoors, Leah was just getting up. Through the ceiling I could hear her humming to herself as she got ready for work, and soon she appeared, still humming, at the foot of the stairs. She was suprised to see me up and dressed.

'I thought you'd be having a lie in,' she said. 'Your bus doesn't leave till half ten, does it?'

'Couldn't sleep,' I said. 'You know how it is, new job and all.'

'And what a job, eh? Our Ben a policeman! My, those criminals had better watch out now, eh, Mum?'

Mum, sitting in her chair as usual, smiled but said nothing. Inside she was wrestling with apprehension. And who could blame her? Here was her only son leaving home to start what amounted to a new life. But more than that, it was a life that would know danger – even the risk of death. It was no use trying to play these things down, as though they hardly ever happened. The radio and the newspapers told a different story. There was an IRA campaign going on. Policemen were being killed.

But even on that last morning, Mum never said a word to discourage me. She knew that at nineteen I was responsible enough to be making my own decisions, and she would not seek to preserve the life she had nurtured from the womb by holding it to herself any longer. She was a good and wise mother; she knew that I had my own life to lead. Besides, long ago – many years before I had told her of my ambition to join the RUC – she had committed my life to God, and she knew that I too now loved the Lord. If this was the way he was leading me, how could she interfere? There is no safer or better place than the palm of God's hand.

Soon Leah was away to work with a kiss and a smile and a 'Don't forget to write!' And even after that there was still plenty of time before my bus was due. Out in the scullery I ate a leisurely breakfast and then turned my thoughts to spiritual food. But my Bible wasn't to be found in its usual place at the bedside; Mum, I realised, had packed it along with all the other things so thoughtfully got together. It must have been painful for her to do that, making her way stiffly up and down the stairs as she gathered my things, but it was something she wanted to do – a final expression of the loving care which had filled that home ever since I could remember.

In my sister's room I found her book of daily Scripture readings and settled down to see what God would say to me that morning. I suppose I was hopeful for what we Christians call 'a word from the Lord'. I wasn't disappointed. In words that couldn't have been more meaningful if they had been written in the sky, I read: 'Trust in the Lord with all thine heart and lean not unto thine own understanding. In all thy ways acknowledge him, and he shall direct thy paths.' I knew the verses well; they came from Proverbs chapter three. But never had they been so challenging, so encouraging, so heartwarming. What better text for anyone to take with them on a new venture!

At last it was time to get into my overcoat and be on my way. Without too much fuss – for this parting was a painful one for both of us – I kissed Mum, gave her a quick hug, picked up my case and carrier-bag, and stepped out into the world.

At the end of the street I stopped and turned to look back. The winter sun was polishing the windows and shining the grey-slate roofs as the little terraced houses huddled together, leaning on one another against the spiteful wind. In this gentle light Craigwell Avenue

28

looked its best, but even that was nothing to celebrate. But you get fond of a place.

Then the wind came rushing up and lashed me with its icy whip as though driving me on. I turned up my collar, glanced again at home and Mum's face behind the frosty glass, and went for the bus.

Anyone making his way through a little market town in Ulster with a suitcase under his arm in mid-winter is a sure topic for conversation among the locals. On the way to the bus depot in Market Street I must have met or seen just about everyone who would be glad of a bit of gossip.

'And where be you off to, young Ben?' one would ask.

'The Police Training Depot at Enniskillen, Mr Skinner.'

'Then hurry up and get trained and catch them terrorists.'

'I'll do my best, sir.'

The same conversation must have taken place at least half a dozen times that morning, but I didn't mind; I was glad to feel the support of the townspeople. It gave an identity to 'the public' whom this young man was to be trained to protect. Ordinary, good-living people who wished harm on no one but whose peace and safety were being threatened by a troublesome section of our community who refused to let the past die and would stop at nothing to rid the country of the British and restore a united Ireland. I realised that by enrolling as a policeman I was identifying myself with the British government which the terrorists so loathed, and by this act I was making myself their enemy. That was a strange thought and an uncomfortable one; it brought with it a sense of isolation, and somehow it seemed terribly unfair. I was joining the police force to be a servant of the people, not a soldier at arms. Oh well, maybe this terrorist campaign wouldn't go on much longer. Who was to say that by the time my six months' training was over things wouldn't have quietened down? One could live in hops.

At the bus depot I was delighted to find that I wouldn't be travelling the sixty-odd miles to Enniskillen alone. Another Portadown lad – a fellow by the name of Martin – was also beginning a new career with the RUC today. I'd met him at Police Headquarters in Armagh where together we had sat our entrance examinations. But I'd not seen or heard anything of him since, so to find him waiting for the bus, police travel warrant in hand, was a real boost. When there are two of you the unknown doesn't seem so daunting. In fact, once we got talking about this new life on which we were embarking, our spirits were lifted and before the bus had arrived we were chattering excitedly of our prospects and the days ahead.

Soon the bus shuddered and hissed to a standstill and its door yawned open to cough out one lot of passengers and swallow another. Martin and I humped our cases aboard, pushed them into a convenient corner and settled down in our seats as the unfamiliar journey began. As the bus creaked and growled its way through the town we sat in silence, watching childhood and adolescence slip past the windows, our old lives disappearing in exhaust fumes, our new ones unknown and untouched awaiting us on the shining road ahead.

That was a long and beautiful journey, our eyes filled

with the strange but comfortable sights of our lush, green land, our hearts warming to the call of adventure with every passing mile. There was sadness, too, as we thought of loved ones left at home, of friendly rooms and the security of routines. But the farther south that bus took me, the more convinced I became that, far from having left these things behind, they were journeying with me, strengthening me, protecting and enabling me. They were, in fact, the foundations on which my life was to be built. They were solid, they were familiar, they were reliable. And testing them for the first time that morning I felt safe and secure. Not everyone, even some of those from privileged homes, can say the same. No wonder some lives crumble. No wonder some young people, not unlike myself at that time, take a different road.

Enniskillen is away down in the south-west of Ulster in County Fermanagh, not many miles from the border with Southern Ireland. It is a very beautiful market town set on an island within Lough Erne, and thus it commands generous scenic views. It is also a town steeped in history. Every Irishman knows that it was here that James II's army was beaten off just a year before he was put down by William at the fateful Battle of the Boyne in 1690. That battle, in which the kings' religious principles were bound up with politics, tragically resulted in the Catholics being regarded as inferior. It is the history of these events, now coloured by folklore, which lies at the root of today's troubles.

That afternoon, as the bus chugged into Enniskillen and we tumbled out on to the pavement, I couldn't help being reminded of these things. And as we came to the

31

high, grey-stone walls of the Police Training Depot with its armed guards and security barriers, the troubles which had seemed so remote at the beginning of our journey now assumed a face as cold and hard as the guns in the guards' hands. In one withering moment the reality of what I had done in signing on with the RUC stood before me, harsh and naked. And for the first time I fully understood Mum's silent apprehension.

But it was better inside. In its brisk and tidy way it was a warm and comforting place with erect but cheerful buildings, its towering walls embracing everything and everyone within them.

There were twenty-six of us in the batch of raw recruits which arrived that day. Twenty-six young men, Catholics and Protestants, from varying backgrounds and walks of life, and yet drawn together in one purpose – to serve Queen and Country; to assist and protect the peoples of our land. This common bond quickly dispelled the apprehensions that separate strangers, and soon we were chattering and laughing together over our first meal in the canteen. I suppose for many of us the laughter had more to do with the relief of tension than the quality of the jokes and cracks that flew through the air, but that was a good time: it was our first experience of the comradeship that lay ahead, and, like the welcome meal after the long journey, it tasted good.

After dinner we were separated alphabetically and led off to various dormitories where we were to settle in and, as far as is possible in such a place, make ourselves at home. My bed was by a window which overlooked Lough Erne, and I remember very clearly the first time my eyes beheld that view. It was lovely. The dying sun laid a finger of gold across the quiet waters, and on the edge of the lake great oak trees stood proud in their winter starkness, their strong limbs stretching into the sky, their bony fingers scratching at the chill air. In summer, I thought, this would be a fine view, and then I realised that this window was mine for a whole six months, and that through it I would watch winter yield to spring, and spring burst into summer. If I hadn't already done so, this was the moment when I told myself that Enniskillen was a bit of all right. And I knew instinctively that I was going to enjoy life here.

No sooner had the officer who had shown us to the dorm disappeared than a sense of fun rippled through the room, and soon our laughter was bouncing off the walls as old jokes were brought out for their new audience and the clowns amongst us aired their talents to hoots of joy and the occasional round of applause. These were tomorrow's policemen? It's a good job our townsfolk weren't looking in that night!

Later on my thoughts were brought down to earth as I opened my case ready to unpack. On top of the clothes so expertly packed by my mother's hand lay my Bible. At home I was in the habit of reading this every day. I regularly spent time on my knees, too. But what now? Sharing my 'bedroom' with seven other lads wasn't quite what I was used to. And I'd never been very bold in my efforts to witness of my faith to my workmates. They knew I was a Christian and that I didn't share all their interests, but my testimony at that time had been a fairly quiet one, expressing itself, I hope, in my attitude rather than in any outward declaration of my beliefs. I could do the same here, of course, but that still left the

3

question of Bible study and prayer.

I glanced around at the lads. What would they say if they saw Ben Forde, this beefy young fellow from Portadown, kneeling by his bed? And sitting reading the Bible? Some of them had already demonstrated a lively ability to poke fun and have a laugh at someone else's expense. If I got down on my knees, would I become their latest source of amusement? I was still pondering this some time later, having put off the moment of decision by taking an unnecessarily long time to unpack, when I turned to discover that someone else faced with the same challenge had already taken the plunge. A lad named Dennis, whose bed was by the door, was down on his knees, praying. Another Christian! Encouraged by Dennis's example, and pleasantly surprised at the lack of ribbing he received, I was down by my bed in no time and giving thanks to God for his provision that day – and committing the future into his hands.

As I settled into bed that night, the crisp, cold sheets strangely welcoming, those verses from Proverbs came back to me, and I knew contentment as I realised I had obeyed the Lord's word to me that morning and 'acknowledged him'. And as I thought on this, the promise that 'he shall direct thy paths' filled my heart with quiet assurance and eager anticipation.

As I look back now, I know that life's adventures can be exciting, thrilling, satisfying. But never so much so as when they are shared with God.

The following morning we washed, dressed, breakfasted, got kitted out, and met Sid, our squad instructor, who made it amply clear to us that this wasn't a holiday camp and that we were there to work. A few days later we were all sworn in.

And so began a period in my life on which I reflect with much pleasure. I enjoyed the discipline, the varied programme of training, the academic instruction in various subjects pertaining to the law – and on top of this, like the cherry on the cake, there was sport. Bags of sport. If there was a game going on – football, tennis, cricket, football (I loved football!) – you could count me in! I was in my element. And to think I actually got paid for enjoying myself so much! Amazingly, I was earning more than twice as much here as I was at the printer's – and by comparison that was hard work.

The one thing I didn't care much for was the arms training. It was essential, of course, and it was interesting – there was an element of sporting competitiveness in the target practice which I enjoyed – but I did not like guns. The years of familiarity and use have not changed my mind.

There was good fellowship to be had at the training depot. Comradeship was very strong, with not even the different religious backgrounds of the lads being allowed to interfere with the oneness that was felt and enjoyed. Outside those grey-stone walls the Catholics and Protestants may have been at each other's throats, but inside, as if in another world, labels meant nothing; we were fellows, natives of the same land, comrades in mind and purpose. So it always struck me as odd when, on each Sunday morning, we had to fall in and march out of the gates and down through the town, stopping at each church – the Presbyterian, the Catholic, the Methodist, the Anglican – so that those of each denomination could fall out and enter the building which bore the label which for the remaining six days of the week was forgotten. It was good, of course, that recruits were encouraged to respect the Lord's Day and to participate in worship, but it seemed a great pity that the only area in which our young lives were divided was that of religion. In one sense, of course, when all was said and done, it was to deal with the results of the religious divisiveness and intolerance within our land that we were being trained.

Ah, but if history could rewrite itself.

Personally I used to look forward to Sundays and the visit to Enniskillen's splendid old cathedral. I was fortunate in having had a personal invitation from the Canon to worship there and to take part in the choral and other activities of the church. He came and sought me out during my first week at the depot, having received a letter from the Rector of my church back home to say that I was coming to train at Enniskillen and that he was sorry to be losing me from his choir. At that stage I hadn't done any public singing, but I suppose the Rector thought my voice worthy of a place in a cathedral choir. Well, that's a matter of opinion, but the Canon seemed pleased to have me. The lads who worshipped with me in that ancient building appreciated my presence, too, but more as a source of amusement: I suppose it must have seemed quite funny for them to see me in my white robe and shiny-toed size tens clattering down the stone-floored aisle – a sort of 'angel in hob-nailed boots'!

It was while at the training depot that I first heard of the Christian Police Association. I encountered it in the shape of fine men like Sergeants Bowness and Moffett and Constable Carroll. They were instructors at the depot and were a constant source of encouragement and inspiration to the young Ben Forde. More than once I took a problem to them, and every time I was put straight.

After a while I decided to enrol as a member of the CPA and wrote away to the area secretary, Sgt Tom Kerr. The personal reply I received reflected the cheerful, caring spirit which I have come to regard as part of the key to the success of this organisation. That letter was also to lead to personal contact with Tom Kerr and to a warm friendship which I have valued these past twenty years.

I am very grateful to these three Christian policemen; it was through their counsel and fellowship that, as a young man of nineteen and as a Christian of three years, I began to make some real headway in my Christian life. My morning and evening times with the Lord and his Word gradually became more and more precious to me, and I like to think that this was worked out in the daily routine – on the parade ground, the lecture room, and even in Sergeant Wright's team on the football pitch. For Jesus, I was discovering, is passionately interested in every area of our lives and loves to bring his Spirit to bear on all our activities, so that, as he works through us, others will be drawn to him.

As those six months at Enniskillen began to draw to a close, the question on every recruit's mind was: Where will I be posted? Where will my first station be? Throughout the months I had given the occasional thought to this, and I had often wondered what process was used in assigning recruits to their first post of duty. In early August of 1960 all was revealed, and it was very simple.

Recruits who showed an aptitude for academic duties might be sent to a station where eventually they could be moved into the clerical side of police work. One who displayed a particular ability in, say, the art of dealing with drugs would be posted to a station where that type of case might be dealt with. Another who proved to be physically fit and tough would probably find himself assigned to a border station where the long hours and arduous duties demanded men who could stand up to the rigours of service in an area where there was terrorist activity. And so on.

But whatever one's ability or aptitude, every recruit shared the same desire to be posted to a 'quiet' station, such as in County Antrim or County Down. (During that particular IRA campaign of 1956–62 most terrorist activity was confined to the border areas.) I was no different; I was just like everyone else in hoping that my posting would be to a district where there was a large degree of 'normality'. But, of course, it depended on what I was best at. As I saw it I didn't shine in any particular sphere; rather I looked on myself as a reasonable all-rounder. So on what criterion would this young man be placed?

The answer came one morning when Sergeant Wright took me to one side and asked me if I would mind being assigned to a station in the area – perhaps Kesh, fifteen miles from Enniskillen. Now Kesh was not the sort of place you would choose for your first station – or your second, or third . . . It was close to the border in a sort of outpost situation. Someone who'd seen it said there were sandbags and barbed wire around the station building and the outside walls had grooves in the bricks where

IRA bullets had ricocheted off. When you went out on patrol your knees shook a bit and you wondered if you'd ever be coming back. The thought of all this didn't exactly fill me with enthusiasm. So I asked Sergeant Wright why he thought I should apply for this little corner of hell.

He grinned and said, 'Why, you're the best left-half in the place. I want you in my County Fermanagh side.'

Things were looking up. Maybe those stories you heard about Kesh and the IRA were exaggerated.

I grinned back at the beaming Sergeant.

'When do I start?'

4

Guns at the ready

Sometimes I don't feel like praying,
But He speaks words of love just the same;
And deep in my heart there starts flowing
Living waters, songs of praise to His name.

I travelled down to Kesh on one of those days when the sun and the clouds play tug-of-war, with neither side winning for very long. The weather fitted the mood of the journey, for one moment there would be the brightness of a beauty spot, the next the shadow of a terrorist haunt; on one stretch of road a breathtaking view, on another a place known as trouble. These conflicting sights made a yo-yo out of my emotions as the police Land-Rover sped through the lanes, and my travelling companions – two officers from Kesh who had come to collect me from the training depot – pointed out these various locations. For me the pleasure of journeying through this most picturesque part of our land, known as 'The Lakeland of Northern Ireland', was frequently dimmed as one place after another was identified as potentially dangerous for the policeman.

Our arrival at Kesh Police Station did nothing to relieve the gloom which had crept up on me by the end of the journey. It was just as rumour said: the sandbags and barbed wire were real – only the bullet marks in the bricks were an exaggeration.

After the initial adjustments I quickly settled into the routine of my new duty, but, to my disappointment, it soon became apparent that here at Kesh was little of what I had joined the police force for, and an abundance of those things which did not appeal to me. My cherished vision of serving the people was given a sharp rap on the head as I realised that there were few people here to serve: there was but a handful of houses, a spattering of shops, and mile upon mile of deserted countryside. Even the policeman's role of upholding the law was rarely in demand.

There was still plenty to do, however, but most of it was what at that time I considered to be the work of the soldier: patrolling the border and deterring the terrorist from crossing it to carry out his treachery. This meant long and dangerous hours of scouting – our main occupation at Kesh – during both day and night. We would go out on the road, often in one of the Land-Rovers but sometimes on foot, inspecting and searching every place which could be used by the enemy for an ambush – bridges, culverts, derelict houses – and keeping watch on buildings which were possible targets for sabotage. Our own police station was included, of course, which accounted for the sandbags. Many a day I spent tucked in behind the bags, at my back the police station doors bolted shut against the ever-present threat of attack, and in front the dark thickets and whispering fields which at any moment might explode with gunfire. Distasteful and unenjoyable as this form of duty was to me, I believe my entire experience in the RUC has benefited from those months at Kesh. The very real danger which accompanied every mission – not just the special manoeuvre but every assignment down to the most routine patrol – taught me a vigilance and a careful respect for the enemy which no amount of training could have instilled into me. When, for example, duty called for inspection of an old building, and it was a potential hiding place for terrorists, or the sort of place they would lay a landmine or booby-trap bomb, that building would be approached with the very greatest care, many different types of check being made before it was finally entered and searched.

You never forget that you have to tread on a landmine only once to set it off, and when you know you have but a single chance of escaping death, the quiet fear this generates teaches you to walk carefully. One wrong move, one careless action, could be your last. You are also aware that it is not only your own safety but often also that of your colleagues which could be endangered by your failure to stay alert. I believe the need to do this has served me well.

Sometimes duty called for us to be placed in a very vulnerable position: situations in which your palms would begin to sweat, even on the coldest day. I remember being shaken from my sleep in the early hours of one morning and told to dress quickly: the station at Belleek, twenty miles or so down the road, was under attack and our station commander was sending a convoy of police vehicles to assist. The worst part was being told that it was likely the station had been attacked in order to bring out patrols like our own for the purpose of ambushing them.

I hadn't been at Kesh very long, and as I scrambled

into my clothes I wondered, not for the first time, how I'd let myself in for this nerve-racking, knife-edge existence which seemed to bring new dangers each day. What, I asked myself, could cause a young man with a secure job in a quiet, safe town, and with every weekend to himself, to throw it all up for this? I didn't have time to answer before I was being hustled outside and into one of the Land-Rovers, their exhausts coughing impatiently beneath a black-velvet sky. Orders were barked across the ringing courtyard, doors slammed shut like erratic gunfire, engines revved, gears crashed, and we moved out, tyres squealing, into the deep night. The armoured vehicles led the way with the Land-Rovers and cars following behind, each hanging on to the other's tail. But before the soft lights of Belleek loomed in the sky the convoy was slowing to a crawl and our CO was explaining that we were approaching a potentially dangerous stretch of road – a likely spot for an ambush. Even though there was no time to lose in reaching our colleagues at Belleek, precautions were necessary here; otherwise we may never make it to the beleaguered station.

In the cold stuffiness of our vehicle tense glances were exchanged, but before we could remind ourselves of the dangers more orders were being handed out. By now the vehicles had eased to a halt and one of the sergeants was being instructed to walk ahead of the convoy as it proceeded slowly through the danger area. He was to watch for anything suspicious on the road ahead – such as evidence of a landmine – or any sign of enemy activity along the roadside. This struck me as a particularly dangerous and fearful assignment – just *how* fearful I was to find out when, to my horror, I was quickly despatched

43

to follow behind the sergeant at a distance of about thirty yards.

I think that was the first time I knew the real meaning of fear, for it is one thing to tread carefully around an old building on a routine patrol, but quite another to walk down the middle of a road with the moon, like a lantern, picking you out and setting you up as nothing less than a slowly-moving target for any sniper in the hedge. That's the fear that turns your boots to lead and makes your heart race so fast you think it's going to burst. And yet never once does it occur to you to run away from that situation. They do a good job at the training depot.

There was a rustling in the field to our left, and as one man the sergeant and I stopped and turned our machine-guns in the direction of the noise. We looked at each other, and the sergeant nodded towards the hedge: he would cover me while I went to investigate. If I'd thought my heart couldn't pump any faster I was wrong. To make matters worse, as I stepped towards the field the sound of my boots crunching and scraping on the road was exaggerated by the thin night air – enough noise, I thought, to alert the whole IRA.

There was the rustle again, and I moved in, gun cocked and set to automatic . . . and then a black shape was moving through the night. Cold sweat broke out on my forehead and in my palms, and my mouth dried up as I aimed the gun from my hip and began squeezing the trigger. Suddenly a moon shadow was beginning to run across the open ground – and I eased my finger back, breathing sharply into the cool air with relief.

No cow ever had a luckier escape.

That was the nearest any of us came to using arms that night. There was no ambush, and when we finally roared into Belleek it was to find the station and its officers nursing superficial wounds and laughing the nervous laugh of relief. The terrorist had come and gone, briefly rousing the night from its slumber with another of his angry protests and then vanishing into the darkness from which he had appeared.

Our arrival reminded me of those countless films in which the US Cavalry thunder to the rescue of their besieged colleagues and drive away the marauding Indians at the last minute. Except that by the time we reached Belleek the enemy had decided they'd had enough, or that they were wasting their time, and shoved off. But anyway we hung around looking fierce for an hour or more just to make sure that any lone heroes among them were suitably discouraged. Sure enough, Belleek heard no more of the IRA that night, which for the experienced police officer was just another emergency – but not for me. For me the mission had presented a very personal challenge: if that cow had turned out to be a terrorist, I asked myself as I crawled back into bed hours later, could I have shot him? As I lay there, wishing warmth out of the cold sheets and turning this thing over in my mind, I began to wonder at the thought that I could ever be a source of danger to another human being. I wasn't trained like the terrorist, who kills out of hate and a belief that his political motives justify any outrage. In my whole life I had not known hatred to this degree. Bitterness had no say in my education at school or at home. Instead I was taught to be tolerant and respectful of others' views, reasoning sympathetically with words,

45

not lashing out with my fists and trying to force others to see things my way.

Looking up through the steamy windows, the pale light of dawn creeping across them, I told myself that, had I met a terrorist that night, probably I would have tried to talk to him. But then I had a picture of my squad leader at the training depot shaking his head and saying:

'That's the way to get yourself killed, lad, giving the enemy the opportunity to empty his gun into you while you try to strike up a cosy little tête-à-tête! Give him the chance to surrender, of course, but keep your head down. He won't think twice about blowing it off.'

I didn't get an answer to my question that night. Sleep came stealing up on me and carried me off in its comfortable arms. When I awoke all thoughts of killing had been safely locked up in one of those little corners of the mind. But it wasn't long before I found myself in a similar situation in which the question presented itself again.

I was on patrol with some other officers – you never went out alone – in an area very close to the border. We were searching in the hedges around a field and I was a little way ahead of the others. Suddenly I heard a movement in the undergrowth and immediately suspected an ambush. The gun in my hands was quickly cocked and aimed at the hedge, and in the same second a man broke through the foliage pleading for me not to shoot. He turned out to be a farm-worker who was 'only loosening a button'.

I think he, like the cow, came very close to being shot, and perhaps a more experienced, more hardened policeman would have had his gun emptied into that bush before the man could have identified himself. Certainly we were living and working in an atmosphere occasionally so fraught with tension that such a reaction would not have been impossible. The self-preservation instinct becomes highly developed in these circumstances, and the thought of an ambush is never very far from your mind. As for me, as I mulled this over between the sheets that night, I was more aware than ever that my upbringing was having a restraining influence on my reactions, which was as well for that farm-worker. But what also struck me quite strongly this time was the fact that, had there been any danger to myself or my colleagues, I wouldn't have hesitated to use the gun. That seemed a balanced and satisfactory response to my earlier question, and that night I slept the sleep of the just. From that day to this the same attitude has prevailed in my mind.

Something else which life at Kesh did for me was to physically toughen me up. Being an avid sportsman I was used to a bit of cold weather, and blue knees never used to worry me. But at Kesh we went on some winter manoeuvres that made a bitterly cold day on the football pitch seem like a real treat. Anyone who thought he was tough soon had the smile frozen off his face.

It would begin in late afternoon or early evening – the sort of time when sensible folk were drawing the curtains and settling themselves round a good fire. Our evening was to be spent in a very different way. Kitted out in battledress, and with a flask of soup as precious to us as our weapons, we would set off into the brittle night to defend our cosy countrymen from the terrorist. Like the RUC, the IRA didn't stay home just because there was frost an inch thick on the ground. Whatever the weather – short, perhaps, of a blizzard, when we suspected the enemy didn't fancy venturing out either – we were there under the stars, guns at the ready – if ever our numbed fingers could have found the trigger.

The brief was always the same: patrol such-and-such area, watch for terrorist activity, detain any suspects. As I recall, we never caught many terrorists, but that isn't to say we weren't successful. Our principal role was to deter the enemy from his criminal pursuits. I think the fact that few IRA missions were successfully effected in that area during that campaign is a fair measure of our achievements during that period. Not that that was much consolation at the time. In fact, perhaps if we'd seen a bit more action we may have kept a few degrees warmer. As it was, much of our time was spent standing or lying motionless while the vicious cold gnawed away at our bones. It didn't seem to make a lot of difference to your extremities; once your ears had turned purple or your feet had dropped below freezing point you hardly noticed they were nearly falling off!

We endured some really fierce nights. The coldest ones were always the most beautiful, when there wasn't a patch of cloud and the stars came out in force to mock in majestic silence. Under your feet, or under your whole body if you were lying prone, the iron earth was no more merciful. Worse, if it could drag another degree of body heat out of you it would.

One night – a really cruel, brutal night – we were sent down to Pettigo, about five miles from Kesh, to mount surveillance on the village's handful of buses, parked overnight in a layby (the company had no depot). These buses would have been a typical target for the terrorists' border activities at that time, and even though their destruction wouldn't have made much of a dent in the country's economy or efficiency, it would have been a major blow to a country district like Pettigo.

The site was best observed from the top of a nearby railway embankment. We reached this from behind in early evening, got down on our bellies and shuffled into position to wait. There we stayed, our blood turning to ice, until it was decided, hours later, that on this particular night the buses were in no danger. And so we began to move – or tried to. Our uniforms, we found, had become literally frozen to the ground, frosty fingers having infiltrated our tunics and clutched our shivering bodies to the earth.

We ripped ourselves free, our battledress as stiff as cardboard and as frosty-bright as the stars, and staggered off to our transport in torpid silence, our thoughts running ahead of us to the mugs of steaming cocoa that would gladden our hearts and thaw our limbs. And while we drank beneath the unreal light of dawn and electric bulb, we would yank off our boots, rub the life back into our toes, and tell the lads what a beast of a night it had been. And they'd believe us when we said it was so perishing cold that our uniforms froze to the ground, because last night it had been their turn and it had happened to them.

It would not be honest to paint my life at Kesh in only dark colours. There was much light in the picture. On many days the strain of living with the campaign was barely noticeable and life was lived with guarded optimism. More than that, on a number of occasions we abandoned our cares and downright enjoyed ourselves, usually at times when the terrorists were less active. (Certainly that campaign was not so intense as the one which we have endured since 1968.) On those days, to my great pleasure, it was possible to have home and away football matches with the local Irish Garda, the police force of the Irish Republic, and I also recall many a happy day when we felt quite safe in driving over the border to spend times of welcome relaxation at some of Ireland's very lovely seaside resorts.

Sometimes there was light on the dark days, too – light that came from my times of Bible study and prayer. Not the sort of million-watt brilliance that sees off the darkness and changes the world, but the soft, reassuring glow of a lantern that lights the way ahead and imparts a quiet sense of comfort and security. It came out of the Bible, and it was exactly as the psalmist David described: 'Thy word is a lamp unto my feet, and a light unto my path.'

There was no hesitating at Kesh as there had been at Enniskillen: my Bible went straight on the table the moment I unpacked. God had proved his faithfulness to me through each day at the training depot, and when I arrived at Kesh it was with the confidence that he would be with me here too. Of course there were bad days – days when I would fall into bed, exhausted and disillusioned, and wonder where God had been, because he certainly hadn't been with me – but gradually I learned that the problem was with myself, not God; he had been there all the time, and my failure to acknowledge his presence and take hold of his hand was because of my own stubbornness or sin. Generally, though, the fellowship I shared with the Lord was unbroken, and through it I was aware of a peace which provided the antidote to some of the darkest hours.

Making Christian friends was a boon, too. There is nothing on this earth to equal Christian fellowship – it is a taste of heaven – and at Kesh I was fortunate in meeting some fine Christian people. There was the bank manager who led the local Christian Endeavour group; his lively testimony was a great encouragement to me. There were various folk from the parish church who befriended me. And there was the Methodist minister with whom I sought to start up a Bible class in the police station, and through whose godly influence I became involved in the Life Boys youth organisation. Through this and other community activities I found an outlet for the service I was keen to render to our people, and I remember those days as giving me much satisfaction.

For me, Kesh lasted only six months, after which I was transferred to the station at Pettigo five miles down the road. It also happened to be right on the border, which meant we had to be more alert than ever. But the duties were identical to those I had known at Kesh: it was the same endless round of patrolling, searching, and hopefully deterring the enemy by our presence.

A year or so later, home began to call. My mother's health was deteriorating, and, despite the regular contact through letters and the occasional visit, I felt very strongly the great distance between us. Ever since I had been away I had known a sense of responsibility towards my parents, and now this seemed to be increasing. I wasn't very long in making up my mind to request a transfer to somewhere nearer home, and the cheering news came through one wet Tuesday morning: I would be moving to Comber in County Down, not thirty miles from Portadown.

It was to be a move that would herald many changes in my life.

5

Down come the sandbags

You ask me how I know my God is real,
Well, I can't prove it, but I can tell you how I feel:
He took the fear that enslaved me,
And in its place He gave me
Happiness my heart just can't conceal.

Comber is a gentle market gardening town perched on
the shores of Strangford Lough. Like Enniskillen on
Lough Erne, it possesses that deep calm which you often
find near water, as though the secret of the untroubled
depths has overflowed into the streets and come to rest
on the people.

I blew into Comber along with the autumn leaves one
Monday morning in October, 1962, and was immediately aware of its peacefulness, as though, like a contented kitten, it lay softly purring in a comfortable lap.
The tidy houses wore clean faces, and the windows
winked in the morning sun as though they knew something I didn't. What I did know was that, as far as police
work was concerned, Comber was everything Kesh and
Pettigo were not. The troubles down south had barely
touched this beautiful place; there wasn't a sandbag in
sight, doors stood confidently open, and even the air
hung unstretched and unperturbed. It's true that at this

time the IRA campaign was beginning to wane, but I couldn't help feeling that even if there had been a dozen bombs going off down on the border, Comber would have but blinked, adjusted its smile, and gone on being relaxed, welcoming, and bright. And as the hurrying wind bowled me along Killinchy Street and up the steps into the police station, I smiled to myself and savoured the sweet taste of normality.

There were more pleasant surprises inside. There was a homely sort of atmosphere about the place; a caring warmth that you don't normally associate with police stations. I soon discovered the reason why: Sergeant Barker, who was in charge, and his wife Eileen were Christian folk. Their love for the Lord was channelled into their service for him here in the station, and there wasn't an officer in the place who wasn't embraced by that love. For me, of course, this had a special meaning; it was the nearest thing to the love of home I had known since leaving Portadown. Living in at the station meant that I received the full benefit of this love, right down to frequent helpings of Mrs Barker's chocolate cake – her speciality. It was all a long way from the nerve jangling of Kesh . . .

As I got into the stride of my beat over the next few weeks I began to unwind. It felt good to be able to walk down the street without six pounds of gun-metal in my hands; good not to have to keep glancing over my shoulder; good to be able to walk in a dark place without wondering if I might step on a mine. But best of all it was good just to be a policeman. At last I was doing the things I had always wanted to do. Helping, exchanging a cheerful word, imparting a sense of security . . . simply being of service to the people.

Quickly accepted as part of the community, I was soon into various social activities – the youth club, the tennis club, the football team – but it was in the area of Christian fellowship and service that I was to find the greatest satisfaction. Encouraged by the sergeant and his wife, I found myself making many new friends in the churches and fellowships in the area, and the times spent with these folk were an inspiration, building my faith and deepening my knowledge of Christ as my Saviour, Lord and Friend.

I suppose everyone who knows Jesus can look back and point to times in their lives when they took a major step forward or turned an important corner in their Christian experience. For me such a moment came shortly after I had moved to Comber. Comber was a sub-station with its headquarters at Newtownards, and every now and again the Head Constable of the division would visit the sub-stations to make the required inspection.

The first time I met this man – his name was Walter Allen – I discovered that he too was a Christian; he talked openly and gladly about his faith in Christ, and, having learned that I too acknowledged the Lord, he was quick to express fellowship with me. Rank structure didn't come into it; we were one in Christ.

He had an infectious enthusiasm for his faith, and I recall with gratitude how he exhorted me to get to grips with the Lord. He described Christianity – and I believe he was fond of quoting this – as something like swimming. 'Put a foot in at a time and it's cold,' he would say. 'But jump in and you enjoy it.' With his help I was about to 'jump'.

He did quite a bit of public speaking, and still does, proclaiming the message of the gospel from the rostrum or pulpit, and on one occasion when he was due to address a Youth for Christ rally at Killyleagh, eleven miles from Comber, he asked me if I would care to go with him and, if I wished, say a few words about my faith as a young policeman. He wouldn't push me, but would give me the opportunity during the meeting to join him on the platform. When the moment came, complete with butterflies playing leapfrog in my stomach, I nodded my decision to him. To be honest, it wasn't something I longed to do – speaking in public for the first time is nerve-racking – but I felt this was something God wanted of me, and that I would be denying him if I let the opportunity slip by.

As in so many other areas of life, the anticipation was more uncomfortable than the experience, and afterwards I felt that this brief, simple act had been of great benefit to me. It gave me a sense of identity as a Christian – never before had I outrightly confessed my faith in Christ – and during the ensuing days I became aware of the effects of Christ's words to his disciples: 'Whosoever shall confess me before men, him shall the Son of Man also confess before the angels of God.'

The practical outworking of this promise means that where there is obedience there is blessing – the same lesson I began learning at the training depot – and having tasted that blessing I gradually became more and more keen to testify for Christ and joined with other young Christians in Comber as they went out to tell others about Jesus in youth clubs, on the streets, in coffee bars – wherever there were people who would listen.

Of course we had our disappointments, our awkward moments, our failures, but I like to think that I learned fairly quickly about public speaking. Certainly I felt that this was something I could do. It was a positive expression of Christian allegiance and brought a sense of fulfilment and achievement. And I was finding that, just as in the football matches I continued to enjoy, there was more satisfaction to be had from being on the field in the centre of the action than there was in sitting on the side-lines waving a flag.

Inevitably, my increasing desire to share what Jesus meant to me – and he meant more as the days went by – spilled over into my work. From time to time, in the course of my duty, I would take the opportunity to recommend my Saviour, particularly to folk whose circumstances revealed that they would benefit from the loving and restraining influences of God's Spirit in their lives.

The Spirit was also at work in my own life. Through times spent with the Bible, or simply as the result of daily experience, he was fathoming new depths in my soul, teaching me new and stirring truths about Christ, and strengthening my love for him.

It was about this time that I realised I could express this love in another way: through song. One of the other lads at the station was frequently to be heard strumming out tunes on a guitar when he was off duty, and this instrument appealed to me so I asked him if he would teach me. He instructed me in a few basic chords – on which I haven't improved much since! – and, having bought my own guitar, I set to learning some of the old gospel songs. On many an evening I would sit in the station and sing these songs, accompanying myself in faltering style, but thoroughly enjoying myself.

I hadn't been doing this long when Mrs Barker asked me if I would sing during one of the services at the Methodist Church which she and her husband attended. I readily agreed, and a few days later, on a Sunday evening, I got up and sang my first song in public. It was 'In Times Like These (You Need a Saviour)'. It was one of the first songs I learned on the guitar, and in view of the recent troubles it seemed appropriate. It had a message for me too: times were coming when I was to learn just how much 'I' needed Jesus.

From that night on I received various opportunities to sing the gospel, mostly in churches or at fellowship meetings. But occasionally a request would come from an unusual quarter. There was no more surprising invitation – although it was more of a challenge – than the one I received late one Saturday night. I had gone down to the café by the cinema to get some supper for another young, unmarried officer who lived in at the police station. (The pair of us more or less existed from chip shop to café at that time.) The pubs had long since closed and tipped their customers out on to the street, and a number of them had found their way into the café where, their tongues loosened by the evening's beer, they were belting out a boozy version of some Irish folk songs.

While I was waiting to be served, and during an interval when the singers were trying to decide which song to murder next, one of these men, who evidently knew that I was a Christian and sometimes sang gospel songs, looked across at me and suggested in a liquid voice that I favour them with a hymn.

I was in uniform at the time and smiled and said good humouredly: 'Look, boys, I'm on duty. I can't sing now.' Instantly the reply came back: 'You should never be ashamed to sing the gospel of Jesus Christ.'

I hadn't expected that. It put things in a different light. I considered the situation for a moment, then said: 'All right. Just this once.'

And so there in that packed café, amongst the steaming meals and under a cloud of burnt fat and cigarette smoke, I let them have the song I knew best, 'In Times Like These'.

To begin with I felt somewhat embarrassed – I wouldn't have done this unless I had been pushed – but gradually I became aware that, one after another, the late night diners had stopped eating and were looking at me in silence. Even the waitresses had come to a halt in the aisles between the tables.

By the time the song was through I felt pretty good – here was an opportunity the Lord could use, I thought – and then I was into another favourite of mine, 'How Great Thou Art'. Again, I had everyone's attention. Whether it was the unlikely sight of a uniformed policeman singing his heart out in a café that held them, or whether the words of the songs were reaching them, I don't know. But they all listened.

When I'd finished I looked at the man who had challenged me to sing – and either his supper didn't agree with him or something else was getting at him; he looked most uncomfortable. I sensed it was the words of the songs which had disturbed him.

I knew him simply as Ronnie and I knew he lived not

far from the police station, so when I'd got the supper I had come for I suggested we walk up the road together. I wasn't surprised when he eagerly agreed.

As we made our way slowly up the main street, leaving behind us the distractions of the café and the beery-breathed songs, his story came tumbling out. He had once been a committed Christian, but over the years, through various circumstances, he had fallen away. Recently God had been speaking to him. Tonight, said Ronnie, he felt as though he was being called back.

When we parted that evening it was with an arrangement that he should accompany me to church next morning. We went together many weeks from then on, and we became quite good friends. Eventually the day came when he echoed the words of Psalm 51: 'Restore to me the joy of thy salvation', and through a prayer of faith he was re-established in his relationship with Jesus. Not long after that his sister became a Christian too, and from there on they went on with the Lord.

Not so long ago, Ronnie died suddenly. But he died with the song of the Christian in his heart, rather than the empty words of the folk song on his lips. I often wonder whether that would have been so, had I refused the lads a song that night.

One morning I was lying in bed, having just turned in after the night shift, when the officer on duty at the desk came in and told me there were a couple of girls down-stairs who were asking to see me.

'But I've just got into bed,' I protested.

'Then just get out again,' he said – and added, wink-ing: 'Besides, they're a couple of good lookers.'

So I pulled on my tired uniform, ran a comb of fingers through my hair, and went down. He was right about their looks.

Both, I quickly discovered, were named Elizabeth, but to make matters easier one was known as Lily. They had heard me speaking at a meeting some while back and wondered if I would address their Christian fellowship. I said I'd love to. We had a bit of a chat before they left, and then I went back to bed, making a mental note to mark the engagement in my diary . . . and thinking what a lovely girl that Lily was.

Up until that time I hadn't given much serious thought to girls. I'd had the occasional date when I was at the printer's in Portadown, and there had been girlfriends whilst at Enniskillen, but since receiving my first posting I had been working hard at my new career, and my spare time was devoted to my sporting interests, various Christian activities, and keeping in touch with home. That didn't leave much room for Cupid. But that was before Lily came on the scene. And as I snuggled down into bed that summer morning in 1964 I couldn't help smiling. How long was it till that fellowship meeting?

When the day came, I whistled my way through my work, gobbled down my tea, dressed in my smartest clothes, and combed my hair at least half a dozen times. Then I was on my way in the old Renault I'd bought when I moved to Comber.

But there was disappointment awaiting me at the end of my journey: Lily wasn't there. And later that night, having said my piece and sung my songs, I left the church with my smile just a little tarnished. Lily, I learned, had a boyfriend.

61

'Pity,' I said to myself out loud as the Renault spluttered and wobbled its way through the familiar streets. 'Ah well, you can't win 'em all, Ben. Anyway, it's football tomorrow.'

But somehow at that moment I couldn't work up my usual enthusiasm for my favourite sport.

It was Christmas before I heard any more of Lily, and by that time I'd forgotten – well, tried to forget – all about her. Her sister Renee's twenty-first birthday was coming up and Lily had taken on the job of organising the games for the party. She had an idea that they might go off better if someone who was used to public speaking were to handle this side of the event. And she thought of me!

Starry-eyed and hopeful, I went along armed to the teeth with all the games I could lay my hands on, and wishing for success in more ways than one.

As my eyes met Lily's for the first time in the church hall that evening my resolve was strengthened; she did not look away. The boyfriend noticed this and, realising the challenge, picked up the gauntlet. That night, between the paper chases and guessing games, and in and out of the cheese-straws and banana trifles, battle was done, the knights of the oblong table fighting it out for the hand of the fair maiden. First he would lunge with a quick cuddle, then I would parry with a bit of cheery chat; he would come back whispering sweet nothings in her ear, and I would be forced to bring out my biggest grin and cheekiest wink. And so it went on, and me having to keep the party moving at the same time! But I won. I won! After the party my opponent took Lily home, and once more was allowed to hold her hand, but he no longer held her heart.

That night – a crisp, invigorating Saturday night – the moon and stars came out brightly to cheer me on my way, and the Renault and I sang our hearts out as we sped joyously home on the silver road.

I didn't have to worry about asking Lily out; she asked me – in a roundabout sort of way. One afternoon the following week Renee came into the station on the pretext of gathering information for a treasure hunt. We got chatting and she 'happened' to mention that the next evening she and her boyfriend, along with Lily, planned to drive up to the seaside town of Newcastle.

'Oh,' I said, falling headlong into the sweet trap, 'is anyone going with Lily? I mean, will there be just the three of you?'

She smiled cheekily. 'That's right. Why? Fancy making up a foursome?'

The following months were full of happiness, fun, and magic 'goodnight' moments in the drive of Lily's house. But what gave special meaning to our relationship was the fact that underlying our courting was a sense of God's blessing; a sense that he had brought us together and that he was behind the love that was growing between us.

God was at work in Comber in other ways too. As though suddenly switched on, more and more Christians were finding the God-given power to go out with the gospel and to help many people find their way to a new life in Christ.

Lily and I had the privilege of being part of those exciting times, for we found that, together with Renee and Lily's other sister, Rhona, God was using us to take the message in testimony and song to numerous places where there were people, young and old, who hadn't the joy of knowing Jesus.

I particularly recall our visits to the borstal in Millisle. Clearly God opened up a way for us and other Christians to enter this place and have the inmates brought together while we sang and spoke of Christ's victory for the sinner on the cross. These were very informal evenings – we were neither organised nor polished – but they seemed to be appreciated, and I well remember how some lads' mouths dropped open and they stared wide-eyed and glad as they heard about 'God's Free Pardon'; and how, as we shared coffee and biscuits with them afterwards, they would pour out their questions. Over the months a number of those lads claimed that pardon for themselves through faith in the Saviour, and then began spreading the word to their mates.

On many occasions we went with Lily's father, Robert Patton, to take gospel services in the area. Robert was, and still is, a fine preacher, and time after time God honoured the faith behind our words and songs, using them to reach many people, meeting each one at their point of need.

A measure of the extent to which God was drawing people to himself was the size of the crowds attracted by the open-air meetings in Comber Square. Organised jointly with Comber's Christian policemen, these were so popular that they required police supervision to prevent the crowds from blocking the streets and bringing traffic to a standstill.

The response we saw to the gospel during those months had nothing to do with us or any other Christians; we weren't special. The fact was that God had chosen that time to visit the people in that part of Northern Ireland. We just happened to be fortunate enough to be there, ready and willing to be used for his purposes.

As a result, we Christians were blessed too, for blessing has a way of rebounding. Like the widow of Zarephath who served God by feeding Elijah during the months of drought, we found that as we emptied our cups in service to him, so he filled them up again to meet our own needs. But God, I have discovered, does not always act simply to supply the need of the moment; often he is looking much further ahead. Although I could not know it at the time, for me those tremendous months in Comber were a period of preparation for the years to come. They were times of much light in our land. I believe that through them God was equipping me for the darkness we know today.

Before the long night of troubles was to befall us, however, God was to take me through a dark cloud of personal sorrow.

Throughout my time in the police force I had kept in close touch with home, exchanging letters with Mum each week. Although I was now much nearer my folks than I had been in my first postings there was still sufficient distance between us to warrant that weekly letter. I looked forward to it.

One morning in April, 1966, the envelope bearing Mum's familiar, pained handwriting contained much more than the usual chatty news: it was a letter of thanks. Mum had written to thank me 'for all the happiness you have given me as a son'. It was not the sort of thing she would write normally, but she said this was on her mind and she wanted to express the thought while it was fresh in her heart.

However close a man has been to his mother it is hard for him to respond adequately to such sentiments. But a few weeks later, three or four more letters having passed between us, I sat down and wrote, in a young man's awkward way, my appreciation of Mum's love for me. My words were not as eloquent as hers, but the meaning, I hope, was just as rich.

A week later, while I was on desk duty in the early hours of one morning, the telephone rang and it was my Aunt Winifred who lived two doors down from our home. Mum was bad and had been taken to the hospital in Lurgan just a few miles from Portadown: could I come right away?

I went and woke Sergeant Barker and told him the news.

'I'm sorry to hear that,' he said, and got out of bed. 'Of course, away you go, straight away. Get home as fast as you can.'

The old Renault, its pistons beating their hardest, whisked me through the harsh night beneath a busy sky of blustery wind and ragged cloud. We travelled fast and furious, but despite the empty miles the journey seemed endless, until, at last, the dark, beckoning shapes of Lurgan came into view.

Dad was there by Mum's bedside, with my Aunt. By this time Leah was working with the Church Army and living in London; she was to come over a day or so later.

It was a stroke. It paralysed Mum down the left side of her crippled body.

When I saw her, unconscious and clean and frail and white, I remembered the night she darned my school socks by candlelight because there was a power cut. I used the candle's yellow glow to make shadow-figures of funny rabbits and fluttering birds on the wallpaper. I was only six and she was suffering even then.

Mum died a week later. She never regained consciousness.

Lily was marvellous. We had become engaged a few months earlier, and now, through the weeks of sadness, the Lord showed me what a wonderful partner he was giving me. It wasn't just her love and compassion which meant so much to me at that time, but also her ability – or perhaps it is a gift – to sit down and talk when talking helps.

Late one night, after we'd been out for a drive, I pulled up outside Lily's house and turned off the ignition. We sat there for some time, looking straight ahead and saying nothing. After a while I cleared my throat.

'You know,' I said, 'as you look back, you begin to see how God's plan has been working out in your life. I mean, like when I requested the transfer from Pettigo and was given Comber. Transfers were hard enough to get down there – but to be given Comber . . . Well, I just couldn't get any closer.'

Lily said, 'You mean that God was behind it? Because he knew about your mum; knew you'd need to be close?'

I nodded. 'And there were the letters. It's almost as though she knew her time was running out, so she wrote and told me what she wanted to say while she still had the chance.'

'Do you think she knew?' asked Lily, and gently laid her hand on mine.

'No. No, I don't. I think it was the Lord. Like it was the Lord who prompted me to write back while there was still time.' I turned to Lily and smiled. 'I wouldn't have been able to say those things after she . . . well, afterwards.'

In the soft light of the street lamps Lily's eyes glistened with waiting tears, and she smiled back at me.

'I feel like praying,' she said.

It's the practice in the RUC that before an officer gets married he notifies headquarters of his intention and requests a Marriage Transfer. This is because in practice it has proved to be better for a policeman and his family if he works in an area other than that in which he lives. Because Lily was from Comber it was considered better that we transfer out of the area, so I filled in the forms and sent them off with a prayer: 'Wherever you want us, Lord . . . '

The date of the wedding was set, and as the day approached we found plenty of things to occupy us in preparing for the occasion and for married life. We almost forgot about the transfer. It came through a week before the wedding – and it came as a bombshell.

The words on the paper said: 'Springfield Road, Belfast.'

It sounds quite nice, and once, in the long forgotten past, it must have been a pleasant place. But now there were no two words in the English language which could chill a peeler's soul like Springfield Road. It had a reputation as one of the toughest areas – if not *the* toughest area – in the whole of Northern Ireland. It was the very opposite of Comber. In Comber the policeman was respected and appreciated. In Springfield Road he was disliked and distrusted by a large section of the community. It wasn't that there was any strong element of terrorism in the Springfield Road area at that time; the problem was one of different political and religious factions, and a high rate of crime, with all the unpleasantness associated with it. The rumours and stories which filtered through from that division painted a black picture, so that it was the very last place in which an officer would wish to serve.

I turned the paper over in my hands, looking at the words again and again, as though I had misread th and expected them, on looking again, to change.

What was the prayer I had prayed? 'Wherever you want us, Lord!' How could he do this to me?

I drove over to Lily's after tea, and we agreed it was the worst wedding present any policeman ever had.

Comber's wedding bells rang out for Ben and Lily Forde on 1st April, 1967. April Fool's Day – and certainly the laugh was on us as far as the weather was concerned. Instead of the hoped-for spring sunshine the sky chucked down everything we didn't want: rain storms, blustery winds, even hail stones. It was warm and bright in the church, though, and behind us the old pews shone like new while little boys slid along them, amazed and amused by the strange sight of the ladies' occasional hats.

The ceremony and reception went off well enough, but it was a tiring event for Lily and me, and we were glad to board the plane that was to whisk us to our honeymoon in Scotland. Except that it didn't quite turn out like that. The plane was bad-tempered and doddery, like an old man with gout, and staggered rather than whisked us over the Irish Sea. As if having conspired with the aircraft to make sure that the honeymoon got off to a bad start, the weather in Scotland was as bad as in Comber – wet and miserable – and Lily and I spent the whole damp taxi journey from the airport trying to convince ourselves that somewhere outside the liquid windows was a beautiful world of soft, green hills and glassy lakes where the sun shone warmly all day. We gave up when we got to the hotel and contented ourselves with a game of mind-the-puddle between the taxi and the front door.

Things didn't go too well inside, either. The manager came breezing up and introduced himself, and then, when it was my turn, I said, 'I'm Ben Forde, and this is my fiancée – er *wife*!'

He smiled politely, but eyed us with suspicion for the rest of the week.

6

Petrol-bombs and punch-ups

I do not mind the rough and winding pathway
O'er mountain steep, thru' valley dark and cold;
It is enough to know He travels by my side
Along the road that leads to streets of gold.

The Springfield Road area is one of Northern Ireland's
living time-bombs: it has all the ingredients of an
explosive situation, and you never know when it may go
off. It is a predominantly Catholic working-class area
bordering on Protestant sectors, and from time to time –
perhaps more frequently now than ever before – tensions
snap and conflict breaks out. There have been times in
its history when the two factions have lived at one, but
when I set foot on that patch in the spring of 1967 it was
with the cold realisation that once again trouble was
beginning to brew. Political and religious bigotry was
once again rearing its ugly head in both quarters, and
hatred and violence were in the wind.

I was thrown into the deep end more or less from the
moment I reported to my new Inspector, not because
he was a hard man but simply because he needed every
officer he could lay his hands on. Even with over fifty
men operating from Springfield Road there were not
enough to cope with the volume of crime and civil dis-

turbances in this tightly-packed two square miles of downtown Belfast. The situation was made worse by the people's attitude towards the policeman, which generally was one of non-cooperation; here, on certain occasions, he even encountered a degree of open hostility.

For me this duty was a baptism of fire into areas of police work which I hadn't touched on before. I found myself involved in the pursuit of criminal suspects, in breaking up street fights, in making arrests in what were sometimes dangerous situations, in riot control, and often in intensive patrolling in order to keep rival groups apart.

It was a tinder-box situation. The air was impregnated with inflammable feelings which needed but a spark to ignite them, and often that spark would be generated simply by friction, such as when a crowd of Protestants had to pass through a Catholic area on the way to a football match. One group would provoke another, stones would fly in retaliation, and within minutes the street would erupt in bitter violence.

The policeman would have to try to separate these factions and as a result often got caught in the middle.

Every officer who has served at Springfield Road has known the terror of this type of incident, and each has his own story to tell of narrow escapes or times when he wasn't lucky enough to get out of the way and caught the full force of the mob's vicious disregard for the law.

I had my own taste of this defiance of the RUC man at about two o'clock one morning when I was on the beat, heading down the Falls Road on my way back to the station. On the corner of Lower Clonard Street a group of men stood talking and laughing noisily; in the policeman's book they were being disorderly.

I crossed the road and approached them under the lone light of one of the few street lamps to escape the attention of the vandals.

'Okay, quieten down, boys, and go your separate ways.'

I'd no sooner said the words than they were on me. There were five of them and they kicked and punched and dragged me along while I did the best I could to defend myself. With each blow my cries rang up the hollow street, but it made no difference; no one but another policeman would have come to my aid, and there was none about.

I was fortunate in that it was winter and I had on a heavy-duty police overcoat; this at least lessened the force of some of the blows. But they didn't spare me; between them they gave me the worst hiding I'd ever had. Even now it hurts to think about it.

When they'd had their fun they cleared off up an alleyway and left me crumpled and sore in the road.

The damage amounted to a couple of tender ribs and a dented ego. But I'm grateful this took place then and not now. Today I doubt if I would come out of that sort of encounter alive. But of course today policemen don't walk down the Falls Road alone; in fact, it is now very rare for an officer to tread that beat – almost all patrolling is done in vehicles. On the odd occasion when a policeman does walk along the Falls, it is with a police Land-Rover fifty yards in front of him and an army Saracen fifty yards behind. (This close co-operation between the RUC and the British Forces is typical of the measures which have become necessary in protecting the lives of those seeking to maintain law enforcement in Belfast.)

When we returned from our honeymoon, Lily and I had set up home in Erinvale Avenue in South Belfast. The house was a modest little semi-detached with big, gaping windows and a shiny, red-tiled roof. There was a garden back and front, but it never saw much of me; our over-stretched force meant long hours for everyone. The job makes demands on the policeman's wife, too, and from the first day I started at Springfield Road Lily was left in no doubt as to the consequences of her marriage: my first turn of duty was a month on nights. The newly married girl who can spend her first nights in Belfast alone and not express fear or apprehension is a good ally to a police-man, a good wife. Lily is a good wife.

In January of the following year Lily went into hospital and returned home with Keri, our first baby and a ray of golden sunshine in those cloudy days. I remember the first time I took her in my arms and watched as she wrinkled her little nose at me.

'Well, Keri, my love,' I said, rocking her to and fro, 'what a world you've got yourself born into. It's hardly a place for a sweet little thing like you, do you know that?'

Her reply sent me into a flap which wouldn't have im-pressed my Inspector.

'Lily! Lily, come quick!' I cried. 'She's all wet!'

Our home was within easy reach of a number of city police stations, which meant that I could be moved around within the Division without any domestic up-heaval. There were plenty of moves ahead. The first was in May of that year to Andersonstown. Here I was doing much the same kind of work as at Springfield Road,

74

except that by now the first rumblings of a new terrorist campaign were beginning to be felt and the effects were spilling into the streets. The old hatreds were being dusted off and hoisted aloft, and the Catholic–Protestant divide was once more being opened up by those forces which feed and thrive upon unrest.

Confrontation with the police quickly escalated until we found ourselves under fire almost daily. As in the past the border territories, like the Falls Road, Shankill Road and Crumlin Road, became the battle grounds, with the RUC having to suffer attacks from both Catholic and Protestant mobs. Bricks, stones and bottles were the favourite missiles. As they hurtled through the air we would take cover behind the vehicles which had brought us to the scene.

As the attacks became more and more fierce we changed from our regular caps into helmets, and when these proved inadequate the shields were brought out. As if all this wasn't frightening enough we had to take our courage in our hands and charge at the mobs in an attempt to disperse them.

Things started to get really scarey when the petrol-bomb appeared out of the sky. If you were lucky you would see it coming and be able to get out of the way. If you weren't and it landed near you, smashing open and exploding with a horrifying 'whoomph!', you could get caught in its river of fire – your own personal hell which left you raw and trembling and sick.

Before long the petrol-bomb was joined by the bullet, and then everyone knew for sure that the terrorists were back; that the IRA were in business again.

During the late summer of that year I began to find myself taking an interest in the CID investigation aspect of
our work; making inquiries, following leads, figuring
out motives and tracing links appealed to me, and I was
to discover that I had a certain amount of natural ability
in these areas. My superiors became aware of this too,
and before long I was hanging up my uniform and starting out on plain-clothes work. Not that I had been
officially appointed to the CID branch – as yet I hadn't
even been given an 'apprenticeship'; I'd have to work for
that. But for the present I was out of uniform.

Lily was relieved, and I suppose I was too. The uniform
marked out a man as a potential target for the sniper's
bullet – the latest threat to the RUC officer, the UDR
man, and the British soldier. But soon I was to learn that
my new duties would bring their own dangers; I would
be treading on the terrorist's ground. There you must go
lightly.

Bank robberies, shootings, fraud, car thefts – these
were the type of cases I was now involved with, and
although on the surface most of them appeared to be
straightforward criminal investigations, a number
turned out to have terrorist connections. The proceeds
from bank robberies were funding the rapidly gathering
campaign of the IRA and its Protestant counterpart, as
were sums of money being milked from commercial
organisations. Shootings had hidden political motives.
And stolen cars were later recovered after having been
used in bank raids or assassinations.

Our inquiries inevitably took us into the dark under-
world of the various political factions and illegal
organisations, and in a very short space of time we saw

a picture of terror building up in front of our eyes. Instinctively we knew that things were going to get worse. Confirmation came with the start of the haphazard pattern of bomb blasts which were to shake our country, and the cold-blooded murders which were to chill the nation's soul.

Evidently my contribution towards the efforts to solve these crimes was satisfactory because one morning in July, 1969, I was called into the Inspector's office and told I was being put on a year's apprenticeship with the CID, and that at the same time I was being transferred to the station at Lisburn Road.

That year was a busy one for the criminals on the Lisburn Road patch, which meant a hectic one for the CID. It was also a *bad* year for us, and for every member of the RUC, in terms of morale. Through the media came an ugly anti-police propaganda campaign. Whether it was something which just happened or whether it was planned does not matter; what matters – and hurts – is that it was effective in portraying the police officer as more of an enemy than a friend of the peoples of Northern Ireland. The impression was given that disturbances in the streets were actually being caused rather than quelled by the presence of the RUC. It was as though we could do nothing right. Criticism seemed to come from every quarter.

The saddest part was that many people swallowed what the propaganda machine fed them, and the result was that police morale took a dive. No wonder, when even some of our neighbours seemed set against us. At one stage I felt so low I had to go down to the newsagent's where I usually picked up an evening paper and cancel my order. It was one thing to be called 'irresponsible' and 'troublemaker', but I didn't have to read about it.

This state of affairs continued for many months and did much damage, not only to the RUC but to law and order in our land. It also did damage within the home, dashing hopes, destroying confidence, and generally lowering morale. Many of those thus affected were, I believe, simply confused, not knowing what to think or believe.

It is my view that even today our society has not fully recovered from the malaise which struck at its heart in those dark days. For me the only light in the situation was that generated by my faith. This gave me the determination to fight back; the strength to continue to believe in what I knew to be white in spite of what was being painted black.

There were two bright spots in those dismal months: in June, 1970, our second child, Clive, was born, and a month later I received my hoped-for appointment as a Detective Constable in the CID. This meant yet another transfer, this time to the Donegall Pass station in the city centre, but I felt, perhaps for the first time, that my career was now on the move.

Starting with me on that first morning was another young man who had qualified for CID work. His name was Neville Cummings and, like myself, he was a man who had committed his life to Christ. I had known him since my Springfield Road days, although until now we hadn't had a great deal to do with each other.

That morning we found ourselves working in the same

office on the same turn of duty, and from the very first exchange of smiles we were set to become good friends. Of course our like faith drew us together, but it was the job which built the friendship, the closeness.

The terrorist campaign was now beginning to bite, and together Neville and I found ourselves walking with danger, dicing with death almost daily. And there was nowhere that could be called safe; certainly the police station was no sanctuary. Every station in the province was a target and many were attacked, some frequently. Donegall Pass was one of these.

One evening Neville and I were in the office seeing to our paperwork and chatting when suddenly shots rang out and bullets splattered the wall outside. Instantly we threw ourselves to the floor, our hearts racing. I looked across at Neville, little beads of perspiration on his forehead. His face told how close he had come to death. He had been sitting with his back to the window.

Close shaves and unnerving moments were now becoming a familiar feature of the policeman's life. On another occasion I was working near the Lisburn Road while investigating murders in that area. At about one o'clock in the morning a report came through of gunfire being exchanged in the Grosvenor Road/Sandy Row area – probably Protestant and Catholic youths, we were told.

Suitably armed, I went down there with a young uniformed officer to see what we could do, and straightaway, on approaching the area, the bullets from both sides started coming for us. A man can stand so much of this, but when that familiar whine comes so close that

79

the air he breathes starts to get hot he knows it's time to retreat.

Back at the downtown Queen Street police station we gave a rap at the front door – by now no police station in the Province left its doors open – but before we could gain entry there was an almighty bang at the back. The ground shook beneath our feet, and then there was a sickening jumble of thuds and crashes. We cautiously made our way to the back of the station to see what had happened. A 'blast-bomb' had been tossed over the rear wall. The noise of the explosion was out of proportion to the damage it inflicted, but it shook us all up.

One thing about such occasions: at least you don't have to grapple with fear; everything happens so quickly. It's the times of waiting and searching that pummel your courage and put the frighteners on you, for it's those times when you have the moments or the minutes to think about what could happen. Looking for bombs is the worst. One time our squad was engaged in searching for stolen property in a warehouse and suddenly one of the men called out: 'Hold it, I've found a detonator.'

It came like a cold hand on the neck. Inside, fear began gnawing away . . .

But we found nothing. Later, however, we learned that there had been a 60-lb primed bomb. It was concealed in the spare wheel space of a car which, during the course of the search, my colleagues and I had been standing on.

These things are hard to bear. I suffer from no delusions about bravery or heroism; I am simply a man who loves his country and his family and I want to be able to enjoy them. But certain people won't let me; at least, they prevent me from enjoying them with the freedom which is my right, and the right of every individual. And so my life is made difficult. Some of the things I have to do, some of the places I have to go, some of the people I have to meet in the course of my work do not make life any easier or more pleasant. Sometimes they make it downright painful because you find that amongst those who are feeding this unrest – this disease, this cancer within our land – are people you know. Ordinary, everyday people with whom you do business or pass the time of day. People who, outwardly at least, appear the most unlikely candidates for terrorism.

One night in August, 1971, about one-thirty in the morning, I was dragged out of my sleep by the telephone ringing; it was my Inspector. A number of arrests had been made and could I be at Girwood Barracks in Belfast at four o'clock that morning to interview some of these men. He said some other things which somehow made me feel uneasy.

A couple of hours later, as I reported for duty, I realised that a new and disturbing phase had begun in the fight against terrorism. It was called internment.

I had been through the interview procedure countless times, but on this night the words seemed to stick in my throat. I *knew* some of these men. Some had been acquaintances of mine for years. One of them was the mechanic who serviced my car. When he saw me for the first time that night he looked away, embarrassed and hostile.

When I got him alone I said, 'What are *you* doing here? What have you been up to that they've hauled you into this place?'

81

He looked at me blankly, gritted his teeth, and said: 'Don't bother, you wouldn't understand.'

Confused, tired, unshaven, I returned home at two o'clock in the afternoon. Lily saw me coming and opened the door.

'Bad time?' she asked.

'Terrible.' And I told her as much as I dare.

'What does this mean, this internment?' she asked.

'Imprisonment without conviction,' I replied. 'If a man is known to be involved in terrorism, regardless of whether it could be proved, we now have the power to sling him in jail. Of course he goes before a tribunal, but he doesn't need to be convicted before we put him away.'

'Well, thank goodness they've done something at last,' she said. 'Perhaps that will deter some of these people.'

'Maybe. I don't know. But I don't like it. I don't think it's a good move – but these are drastic times; maybe drastic measures are necessary. I saw the figures yesterday: six hundred and thirty bombs so far this year.'

'Plus three last night.'

'Oh?'

'It was on the news. Incendiaries. A supermarket, a pub and a garage.'

'Anybody hurt?'

'One man died, I think. But all three places were gutted.' She turned to me. 'They were saying on the radio about bringing back hanging.'

I laughed shortly. 'That wouldn't do any good – cause more bloodshed than ever. No, they need a change of heart, not a broken neck. Instead of thinking of hanging them up we should be trying to put them on their knees.'

I went to the bathroom and washed my face. As I

towelled myself dry I stood facing the mirror above the basin. I looked terrible and felt worse.

'Dear God,' I breathed, 'please stop this madness.'

The madness did not go away. The following afternoon there was another dose of it.

I was sitting at the desk I shared with Neville, making out some reports and wishing I had my friend's magic touch on the typewriter, when in he walked. He saw the look on my face and my two fingers poised over the keys.

Permitting himself a quick laugh, he said: 'Reports? How many this time?'

'Only three,' I replied. 'Short ones, really.'

'Come off of it,' he ragged, 'you don't know how to write a short report.'

'Well, can I help it if my suspects want to make such lengthy confessions?'

He laughed again and looked over my shoulder and flicked through the pages of my notes.

'All right, move over,' he said with mock impatience. 'You go and get some teas.'

'Neville, you're a decent man!'

'Don't try your Irish charm on me!' he grinned. 'Just get the teas.'

When I returned, Neville was talking to one of our uniformed colleagues. I could see by their faces that it was bad news. Neville saw my enquiring look.

'They brought in a former RUC man last night. Got him on suspected murder.'

I shook my head. 'That's all we need. Do wonders for the image.'

'He had a bit of a rough time of it, apparently,' said the uniformed officer. 'Got kicked out about a year ago after a lot of personal trouble. Women and booze, I think. It's the old story – started getting involved with the para-militaries he met while serving in the force.'

'Wait a minute,' I said, 'what's his name?'

The officer thought for a moment.

'Conway, I think. Yes, Bert Conway.'

A strange sensation ran through my body, as though something inside me had died. The shock must have shown on my face because Neville said, 'Here, are you all right?'

I didn't hear him at first; momentarily my thoughts were elsewhere.

'Huh? Oh, sure, I'm all right. It's just that I know Bert Conway. If it's the same one, that is.'

They stared at me.

'Yes,' I said, 'we trained together. Why, he was in my squad.'

I often sat next to Bert Conway at the training depot. He was a quiet fellow and a decent lad. He could no sooner have shot someone than turned bright green.

But he was found guilty of murdering two people.

They were sectarian killings.

He was jailed for life.

7

'No peelers in heaven'

Oft times the day seems long, our trials hard to bear,
We're tempted to complain, to murmur and despair;
But Christ will soon appear, to catch His Bride away,
All tears forever over, in God's eternal day.

It was a grand evening for a spin in the car. A cloudburst
had left the smooth roads coal-black and glistening in the
late sun, and as we sped out of Belfast, along the back
road to Lisburn and out on to the M1 motorway, the
tyres hissed over the wet tarmac and the engine growled
and purred with each successive rise and fall on our route.

There were three of us – Inspector Jack Craigmile, a
Methodist lay preacher, David McIlwaine, a member of
the Police Reserve, and myself. We were on our way to
Cookstown for a Christian Police Association meeting at
which Jack was to be the speaker and I was to sing solo –
at least, that was the plan until I discovered that David,
whom I'd not met before, was also a gospel singer. He
hadn't done a lot of public singing since recently returning to Northern Ireland after several years in Australia,
but we hadn't gone far before I persuaded him to join me
that night.

As we motored on along the motorway in the direction
of Dungannon and veering off towards Cookstown, the

little car became a rehearsal room as we worked our way through 'Farther Along', 'Burdens are Lifted' and 'It Was Love'.

By the time we rolled into Cookstown we were all set for our unscheduled duet, and when the meeting was over we were clapped on the back and encouraged to 'do it again some time'.

My only interest in singing was as it always had been – that it should point people to the only one who could give them peace in this troubled land. If God would use the duet as he had used the solo then I was pleased to be half a duet.

This arrangement was to be short-lived, however. David and I sang together no more than seven or eight times. But out of those brief months of shared ministry was to come a token of our partnership which would go on working for God long after we had parted.

I always looked forward to Thursday nights. Since Lily had taken up the duties of Captain in our local Girls' Brigade, Thursday had been my night off. It wasn't official – the terror campaign had built up to such a pitch over the years that now, in 1975, the RUC man was never really off duty – but as Lily was committed to her 'Brigade night' I could always find a colleague who was prepared to stand in for me. More often than not Neville volunteered, always taking the opportunity to throw in a crack about my 'baby-sitting' duties.

It was good to be home and relaxing and enjoying my usual Thursday night pursuit – the television. This night I was particularly keen to see a documentary which I'd read about in the paper. Titled 'Sing Orange, Sing

Green', it was to cover the well-trodden ground of the troubles (the Orange of the Loyalists, the Green of the Republicans), but from a musical viewpoint.

As I sat back and watched the colour pictures cascading into my living room I was saddened that the producers evidently could find nothing positive or hopeful to convey to their viewers. As the camera took us into the pubs and clubs of Northern Ireland my ears and eyes were filled with what was little more than anti-Catholic and anti-Protestant propaganda set to music. The saddest piece to my mind, though, was that performed by a little lad with a lovely soprano voice – a voice that could be greatly used for the Lord, I thought. His song, called 'The Provo Lullaby', was directed against the police force and ended with the line: 'There will be no peelers in heaven.' Well, that didn't hurt – it was nothing compared with what I'd had thrown in my face over the years – but it struck me as tragic that at so young an age this lad's head should be filled with such thoughts.

The programme moved on, but my mind was still with the boy. I was thinking how good it would be if, as a policeman, I could answer that song; better still, how good if I could project the Christian policeman's assurance of heaven. And then an idea came to me . . .

The following afternoon, during our lunchbreak, I went with Neville to motor-car showrooms in Dublin Road. Lily and I had saved hard for our first brand new saloon, but I wasn't the least bit mechanical and had little idea about best value for money. Neville, on the other hand, was very practical and knew about cars. Like the good friend he was, he offered to come and look at a few models with me.

On the way there I told him about last night's documentary and the boy soprano, and then I said: 'I was thinking I might make a record.'

He glanced at me and laughed, a teasing look in his eye.

'No, don't laugh,' I said, laughing myself. 'You know I don't reckon myself as a singer, Neville, but I'm thinking that maybe this is something God could use. What do you think?'

He considered this for a moment, then nodded and said: 'There's a place downtown; they make Irish folk records and that sort of stuff. We could call in there later; ask for an audition.'

'Well . . . ' I hesitated, 'I'd like to speak to David about it first. I think he ought to be in on it.'

We reached the giant windows of the showroom and stared in at the cars, gleaming like mirrors under the dazzling spotlights.

Inside, Neville said: 'This is the one you want.'

It was rather plain. I liked the look of another and started fussing round it, making admiring grunts and running my hand along its sleek lines.

But we bought the plain one. I trusted Neville.

David liked the idea of the record, and after we'd prayed about it together and individually I went downtown to see these people Neville had mentioned – the Outlet Recording Company. The managing director, Mr William McBurny, was a most genial and helpful man and seemed interested. Gospel music wasn't exactly

Outlet's thing, but he was very willing to listen to a demo tape and if he and his colleagues liked it they would be prepared to record an album. They would press two thousand discs and be satisfied if they sold half.

On the way home that night I made two calls, one to David to tell him the good news and to ask him to give some thought to which songs we should put on the demo tape, and one to Roxaline Simpson, my music teacher. I had met Roxaline when I was singing at a church in Crumlin Road about a year earlier; she was the pianist. After the service she was kind enough to say she had enjoyed my singing, and honest enough to say it could be improved. She was also generous in offering her own services as tutor. I accepted, and we started the following week at her home in Belfast. Thereafter we met practically every week. I hope my voice has improved since then – if not, it's because of my inability to learn, not a reflection on Roxaline's tuition – but what I know for certain is that I thoroughly enjoyed the Christian fellowship we shared. That alone made every session worthwhile!

I took the long route home. It was now unsafe for a policeman to follow the same pattern, do things the same way and at the same time each day. That was asking for trouble. The terrorist acts in phases and at this particular time he was intercepting the RUC man on his way to or from work. To stay alive it was essential to break the routine.

The survival instinct is a good teacher; during those months I learned various devious ways of avoiding the assassin's bullet. If ever I was tempted to relax my vigil there was always a reminder in the morning paper.

Sometimes it would be a policeman I knew.

'But you'll only go in the Lord's time,' a Christian friend once said to me when we were talking about the dangers of my job.

'That's a comforting thought,' I told him, 'but it's no reason for me to throw caution to the wind. I have to be very, very careful. I don't like living like this, but if I don't watch out for myself I could stop one. I can't expect God to look after me if I'm determined to ignore the dangers around me. If I act responsibly I do believe I *shall* go in his time. But if I'm foolish I'll go in my own.'

The day of the recording – Mr McBurny liked the demo tape! – was just such an example of this need to go carefully. The company's studios were located in an area well known for the dangers it held for the police officer, and when we turned up at ten o'clock on the appointed day we were as careful to bring our guns as we were our guitars. It seems ironic that two men recording a gospel album should do so with loaded pistols in their belts, but that is a token of the seriousness of the policeman's lot in Belfast.

Backing us on that first record were Roxaline – we hired a piano from a music shop – Artie Bowman, Roxaline's brother-in-law, on drums, and Paul Cupples, another of Roxaline's pupils, on bass. David and I played guitar, but fortunately David was a much better guitarist than I – although even he had things to learn and one of the engineers didn't hesitate to butt in now and again to suggest additional chords which might improve the overall sound.

The album, we had decided, was to be called 'Fourteen Melodies of Praise' and the recording of these tracks took all day and a few hours the following afternoon. When it was finished we sat down and heard the tapes played back. To our unprofessional ears it didn't sound too bad – although later we were to realise that it left much to be desired – and we left the studio with a prayer that God would use our efforts.

As this new area of Christian ministry was opening for me, so a long-established sphere of service began to close. Attacks on security officers – policemen and prison officers – were being stepped up, making almost any excursion from home a hazard, particularly if an officer was in the habit of keeping a regular appointment such as visiting a sports centre or attending church services. This was enough to make me think twice about continuing my involvement in the church we had joined in Belfast after setting up home, but my mind was made up for me when, through an informer, I learned that members of a certain Loyalist group had been discussing the view that my life should be ended.

A man gets used to hearing this type of talk, but he disregards it at his peril. He must never treat such information lightly.

When I heard this I went home and began moving our furniture around, relocating various rooms in order to achieve the maximum possible degree of safety within the home. If the terrorist came we would at least be as prepared as was possible.

While we were doing this our pastor and his wife called.

'I'm afraid you may not be seeing so much of me at church from now on, Pastor,' I said, and went on to explain my reasons.

He said he quite understood, and that, regardless of my sustained absence from the services (I had never been a regular attender owing to my duty hours), the church would continue to pray for our family's safety, both our physical and spiritual welfare. I am grateful that this man and the people of our church have been as good as their word.

I believe God can use and bring good out of any situation, however much we may dislike the circumstances, and through this new restriction on my life I found God drawing me more and more to himself through personal prayer and Bible study. But as well as feeding me and meeting my own spiritual needs, the Holy Spirit was teaching me fresh truths which were relevant to the kind of people I was dealing with in the line of duty, especially those whom I had to face across the table in the interview room.

Through my training and experience in the RUC I had been moulded for the job I was now doing. But there was another side to my work for which only God could equip me. He had been doing this over a period of time, for there are no short-cuts in God's training school. As I searched the Scriptures during those months I realised that he was taking me right back to square one, teaching me again the basic realities of which I needed to be reminded if I was to go on being used by him in sharing his love with the terrorist or the common criminal.

'Why bother with such people?' I have heard it said. 'They don't deserve love, only punishment.' I understand folk holding this view, particularly if they or their family have suffered at the hand of the law-breaker, but it is not God's view. God's view is that none of us deserves his love, for each man's heart is as black as the next. As the Bible puts it, 'All have sinned and fallen short of God's standard.' Degrees of sin are relevant only to us; to God, sin is sin, no matter how much of it there is. Even our very best efforts to be good are futile, says God; he likens them to filthy rags. Yes, everyone, terrorist or upright citizen, needs his grace, and thank God there is sufficient grace in his hand to forgive and free from sin the very worst of us.

Sometimes people fume when I relate these truths.

'But we're not like the terrorist,' they rage. 'He deserves all he gets.'

God has shown me his answer to this objection. To these people, as to those who would have stoned the woman caught in the act of adultery, he says: 'Let him who is without sin cast the first stone.'

At one time I had my own difficulties with this. But God helped me to understand that because each of us is born with a rebellious and wayward spirit we each have the potential to become a terrorist, a murderer, a thief, and that it is 'there but for the grace of God go I'.

Then God seemed to say, 'If you, Ben Forde, had fallen as low as the terrorist, wouldn't you be glad to know that I had made a way of escape for you? That my son had descended to the very depths of hell in order to offer you his hand?'

'But these people are my enemies!' I protested.

'Love your enemies,' came the reply.

'But, Lord, they have killed my colleagues . . . '

'They killed my son.'

Since my days in Comber I had been seeking to share

God's love with those I met, but now, as the terrorist campaign intensified, so God seemed to increase my desire to do this. I had to tread carefully, of course; I had to get my priorities right. Whilst on duty my responsibilities as a policeman had to come before my longing to win people for Christ. But the Lord seemed to take care of that side of things. He taught me always to be ready to speak for him, but only to do so when the opportunity was there. There has been no shortage of opportunities, for the sin of man weighs heavy on the soul and the man whose sin has found him out is often eager to learn how he might be unburdened. No matter what a man's background – and terrorism attracts all sorts: the minister's brother, the labourer, the doctor's son, the farmer, the policeman's boy – all have the same need of God. Only their awareness of that need varies.

One morning I went down to Castlereagh to interview a man arrested on suspicion of murder. His name was John McKee. He was used to the procedure; he had been interviewed several times and been in prison before. He was heavily involved with the illegal para-military organisations and was not a man to tangle with; indeed he was feared by many.

We sat down facing each other across the table and I began asking him questions. As we talked I became aware that he was feeling very uncomfortable about his past. He was married and had a family, and I began to challenge him about his responsibilities.

'John, do you realise where your life is taking you?' I asked. 'And your family? By your involvement with these organisations and these deeds you are involving them too, you know.'

Slowly, over a period of hours, he began to see things as they really were, like a drunkard sobering up and finally becoming aware of reality. The reality for John was that to deny responsibility for the crime in question could put his own life in danger, such were the circumstances of this case, and that his family could suffer the same violence which he had inflicted on others.

He had a tussle inside – it was written on his face – but eventually he grasped the nettle. His head hanging low, he said: 'All right, I'll tell you about the murder.'

When he had completed his statement the guilt began to show.

'You know, John, the judge can punish,' I said, laying my hand on his shoulder, 'but only God can forgive and give you peace of mind.'

He looked up at me, baffled, as though he couldn't believe his ears. Few men brought in for questioning expect to hear such talk. But, like others, this man seemed interested; keen to know more.

And so began a conversation which this man never thought he would have in an interview room with a detective. As we talked, Christ entered the room . . .

While he was in prison awaiting trial, John asked if I would visit him, which I did. He had been enthusing to some of the other prisoners about the things we had discussed, and he was wanting to start a Bible class. Could I get him some suitable material?

Of course I did. I also spoke with members of his family to see if there was anything I could do for them, and to share with them John's interest in God's Word. Who knows where such contacts will lead?

By the time the trial came round there was something

of a friendship between us. We sat opposite each other in the court. When he was asked, 'How do you plead?' John replied without hesitation: 'Guilty.'

Then he looked across at me and smiled openly and winked.

John is now serving a life sentence for murder. The last time I saw him the Bible class was going well.

In the atmosphere of hostility, bitterness and frustration which prevails in our land it is impossible to be indifferent; everyone is involved. Sometimes pressures become so great that a person who normally would never deliberately transgress the law finds himself involved in an act of terrorism. Even policemen are susceptible.

Frank was a uniformed member of the RUC who had let his feelings get the better of him: through his contact with the various Protestant para-military organisations he had become involved in an incident which led to serious charges being made against him. When I met him he was being held at Castlereagh. It fell to me to question him. He was fairly co-operative, and once the police business was completed I felt it right to open up a conversation about Christianity. Clearly he was interested. We spoke for quite some time and when we parted, he said he would think over the things we had discussed.

I didn't see him again until some months later. I was down in Lisnaskea, making house-to-house inquiries after a shooting incident outside a builder's yard. One of the doors was opened by a man with a Bible in one hand and a pen in the other. It was Frank. Having been formally charged and suspended from the police force he had sought God's help in extricating himself from the circumstances in which he had become engulfed, and now he was a Christian. With time on his hands while he awaited trial he was determined to get to know his Saviour and was spending many hours reading and studying his Bible.

As we stood on the doorstep and chatted it became clear that he regretted his part in the offence, and from his attitude I realised that the Holy Spirit was at work in his heart.

'I don't know what's coming to me,' he said, 'but I do know the Lord will be with me.'

Such results are very thrilling, but rare. More often than not a word about Christ will be gratefully received but taken no further. Occasionally it will be thrown back in my face. On some occasions there is simply no opportunity to introduce God into the conversation. In such circumstances I am sometimes acutely aware of the other outside forces at work in this world, the forces of evil, and through these times the Lord reminds me of the *real* battle that is going on in our land. Not a battle between Catholic and Protestant, or the terrorist and the security forces, but a battle between the powers of light and the powers of darkness, between God and the devil.

Many people reject the idea of a devil. Perhaps they should have been with me when a young lad of fourteen eyed me with contempt and threatened: 'If I had you in the right place, mister, I'd cut your throat and cut it slowly.'

I don't believe any parent, however bitter or hostile, is capable of instilling such malice into a child. It needs the help of the forces of evil.

I questioned this boy at Castlereagh one afternoon. He flatly refused to co-operate. When I arrived home that evening I told Lily about him.

'Unless God steps into that boy's life,' I said, 'he'll commit murder before he's very much older, you see.'

That night we knelt by our bed and embraced him in our prayers.

8

Tommy

Behold the Man – yes, He even knew rejection,
And every hurt that a human heart can stand;
There He stands, the pathway to perfection,
If there ever was a man, Behold the Man.

Tommy Carson was seventeen years of age. He lived in one of the Catholic quarters close to the Falls Road where giant blocks of flats and brightly-lit shopping centres have risen like the Phoenix from the ashes of the ghettos. These clean but characterless buildings tower over the few remaining rows of back-to-backs, one of which was Tommy's home. His was a drab world of frowning houses with grey net-curtains at grimey windows. The paint was peeling off some of the doors, as though after years of neglect it had finally given up clinging to the woodwork and just curled up and died. Most houses had at least one broken window which was boarded up because it wasn't worth replacing the glass: it had been mended before, but a football or a stone or a bottle had smashed it again, so now it was left to stare out, blind and uncaring, across a street full of windows that had gone the same way.

On the corner of the street was a pub with bricked-up windows and a front door scarred by steel toe-caps, and across the way, on the blank-faced end wall of another queue of defeated houses, someone had painted 'Up the IRA' in dripping red letters four feet high.

On most days this wall propped up a bunch of lads who should have been at work, but the factory where they used to stack boxes was no longer there because a bomb had blown it away.

One of those lads was Tommy.

A couple of years earlier someone had tried to get Tommy to join the Fianna, the junior wing of the Provisional IRA. He said no and it cost him a bloody nose. But it was worth it because his Dad had threatened to do far worse if ever he found that his sons – he had five of them – were mixed up with that sort of trouble. In spite of his surroundings, his Dad was a good and decent man who wanted nothing to do with the war that sometimes was fought right outside his front door.

But now Tommy was seventeen and bigger than his Dad and out of work. One night he and his mates went drinking at one of the many unlicensed clubs on the outskirts of Belfast. When he went to the toilet someone followed him in and asked him if he wanted to join the Provos.

That day Tommy had failed to find work again, and the girl he'd got his eye on had gone off with one of the lads across the street. The morning had started with a row with his Dad. It had been a bad day. So Tommy said yes. The man took his name and address and said he would be in touch.

Next morning he woke up, his head banging like a steam-hammer, and realised what he'd done. At first he was scared, but then he told himself that probably nothing would come of it; it was just talk. But a few days later the man at the club turned up on his doorstep and told him he was in. They would be in touch with a job for him soon.

Tommy wanted to say it had all been a mistake, that he was confused when he had agreed to join, that he wanted nothing to do with them. But he had heard what they did to people who crossed them.

A week passed and a stranger called. It wasn't difficult what they wanted him to do. Just carry a gun. Easy. All he had to do was pick it up from one address and deliver it to another.

Scared to get involved, but even more frightened not to, Tommy said he would do it. He knew it was wrong, morally and criminally wrong, and on the way to collect the weapon he went into the local Catholic church to pray for himself and his family. He had sixty-five pence in his pocket. Fifty pence went on candles.

A week later the gun which Tommy had carried in his trembling hand was used to kill a prison officer who answered his door to two strangers early in the morning.

On the following Monday there was some shooting in the Falls Road and Tommy just happened to be passing by. He dived down beside a car and lay there shaking, convinced the shots were meant for him; perhaps his name had been dragged into some sort of internal feud and one of the para-military groups had it in for him. (Or maybe the IRA had heard that he'd been seen talking to a police officer and thought he'd been passing information. Now they wanted his blood . . .) A bullet came scorching past him and he started to sweat. It was no use running, he told himself. They would cut him down before he'd got five yards. All he could do was to get his head down in as safe a place as possible. With any luck there'd be a police or army patrol round any minute.

He yanked at the car's door handle. It was open. Lifting himself very slowly, he half crawled, half dragged himself into the narrow space between the front and back seats and lay there shivering and feeling sick and praying to God not to let him die.

That's where we found Tommy. Neville brought him in.

I bumped into Neville in the corridor shortly after they had arrived and he told me about it.

'Really got the wind up, this one,' he said, shaking his head. 'He got in the way of a shoot-out in the Falls. But something's getting at him; he's worried sick. My guess is he's been up to something and his conscience is giving him a bad time.'

'Do you want me to make a start?' I offered. 'I've just finished with this character next door.'

'Would you? I'll go and enter the arrest.'

There are no distractions in the interview room. Chairs to sit on, a table for tin-foil ashtrays and elbows, four silent grey walls, an indifferent radiator, a light-bulb, and a small, rectangular air-vent. There are no windows. It is a place of isolation, sometimes desolation, even desperation. A place where, even on the hottest day, a man can feel terribly cold, especially a man with soiled hands.

Tommy sat tucked tight up to the table, his head hanging down and his hands clenched in front of him, his knuckles white.

I settled down across the table and looked at him for a

moment. You get to read a person's thoughts, to judge his state of mind. As Neville had said, Tommy had got the wind up about something.

'Lord,' I prayed in my heart, 'help me to help this boy. Please come into this room and enter our conversation.'

Tommy glanced up at me and then lowered his head again.

'Do you want to tell me why you've been brought in here today, Tommy?'

He sniffed and looked up, his eyes searching mine to know whether he could trust me. The corner of his mouth twitched nervously and fear looked out of the windows that were his eyes.

'You're not gonna beat me up, are you? Please don't beat me up.'

'Why should I beat you up?' I said. 'I don't go round beating people up.'

He looked away.

'Some of 'em do, some o' your lot.'

'Well, I can't answer for anyone else,' I said, 'but I give you my word, I've never hit a man except in self defence.'

His eyes met mine again, searching me out. Was this peeler having him on?

'Why, have you done something that you think deserves a beating?' I asked.

The fear was mingled with guilt now.

'Will you tell me about it?'

Silence.

'Whatever it is, it's got to come out, Tommy. You know that as well as I. If you've done something wrong you must face it like a man and take the consequences.

You'll have to go before the judge and he may punish you. He may even acquit you. But I'll tell you one thing the judge can't do, and that's forgive you.'

I'd touched a nerve. He straightened up.

'What? What d'you mean?'

'I think you know what I mean. If you've broken the law, and I think perhaps you have, then the only way you'll get rid of the guilt you're feeling right now is by being forgiven, and *knowing* you're forgiven. But no man can do that for you. I know someone who can, though. Someone very special . . . '

He leaned forward, his interest aroused. He wanted to know more.

Just then Neville came back; he'd brought some teas with him. He passed a cup to Tommy.

Without taking my eyes off Tommy, I said: 'Well, we're getting along just fine here, Neville. You see, Tommy here is feeling bad about what he's got himself involved in and I was just telling him that there's someone who can do something about that.'

Neville smiled at Tommy, and Tommy smiled back.

'Here,' I protested, 'how did you get him to do that?'

Both of them grinned and all three of us sipped tea through our smiles.

I suppose in spiritual terms Tommy had a head start on some of the people I have interviewed. He believed in God and wasn't slow to turn to prayer in a time of crisis, as was evidenced by his visit to the church before picking up the gun. So he listened readily as I told him about Jesus and forgiveness and the Bible and the Holy Spirit. Neville chipped in too. And Tommy had plenty of questions. Between the three of us we covered quite a bit of ground, and all the while Tommy grew more relaxed, more hopeful.

An hour or so later I suggested that Tommy went and thought over what we had discussed. We would talk again later.

'If you feel you'd like to, pray for God's forgiveness and then invite Christ to come and live in your life,' I encouraged him, and added: 'He will. He always keeps his promise. The Bible says: "Whoever shall call upon the name of the Lord *shall* be saved." '

Neville took him downstairs to one of the cells. When Neville came back he said: 'I'm going to nip off home for some tea now, Ben. I'll be back about six and we'll talk to him again. I think he'll tell us all about it then.'

'So do I. Spare a prayer for him on your way home.'

Just after six o'clock Neville went back to Tommy's cell. When Tommy saw him he stood up and smiled. It was the sort of smile that contained far more than recognition or welcome.

'I did it,' he said, almost with relief.

Neville put his arm round Tommy's shoulder.

'Best thing you *could* do,' he said, and upstairs in the interview room we went on to encourage this lad in the new life on which he had embarked, this freedom he had found in a prison cell.

When I felt the right moment had come, I said: 'Will you tell us about this trouble you've been in, Tommy?'

He looked away and the smile he had worn fell from his face.

'That . . . murder . . .' he began slowly, 'at the . . . pub . . .'

'Last week in Lisburn?' asked Neville.

He nodded.

'Well, I . . . ' And then a rush of words: 'I carried the gun that killed that man.'

Neville and I exchanged glances, then looked at Tommy.

'Do your parents know about this?' I asked.

He shook his head.

'Then I think we'd better get your Mum or Dad down here before we take a statement.'

Tommy's father came down to Castlereagh and I told him all I could, including the decision his son had come to regarding God's forgiveness. Understandably, this man was angry at his son's involvement with the terrorists, but also very relieved that he had made this commitment of faith and decided to make a complete confession of his criminal actions.

In the interview room there were sharp words, comforting arms and regretful tears.

The statement was taken and signed, the formal charge was preferred, and then there was the parting, Tommy to be taken to his cell and his father to be driven home by myself.

Outside it was a clear night, but inside the car a cloud of gloom hung over my passenger.

'What will happen to him, Mr Forde? I mean, what will he get?'

'Well, it's his first offence and he'll plead guilty . . . It's hard to say in these cases – but all the facts about tonight and his previous character will be taken into account . . . Perhaps a short prison sentence.'

'I've got five of them, y'know,' he said quietly. 'Five

lads. Me and my wife, we've tried to bring 'em up right, but it's not easy in this place . . . '

'Got two of my own,' I said, smiling across at him. 'Boy and a girl. Younger than your family, of course, but I know what you mean about bringing them up.'

He nodded, grim faced.

'What makes 'em do it, that's what I want to know.'

'All sorts of reasons,' I said. 'There's the hard-nosed IRA man who's in it because of his convictions, but the majority of them haven't any high ideals about the politics of the thing. Some of them are looking for a cause or an opportunity to take out their frustrations on someone else; others are after kicks. But many of them, like Tommy, get dragged in for one reason or another and haven't the nerve to say no. We've seen them all.

'You know, people think terrorists are somehow different from everyone else, but they're not; they're people like you and me. Some are frightened, some are angry, some are victims of circumstance. They're the saddest of all. I expect you've seen it happen. A man gets into trouble of one sort or another – perhaps his marriage breaks up or he loses his job; he turns to drink or crime – and while he's down the terrorist groups get hold of him. They're snapping up these people all the time . . . '

'And Tommy? What will become of him? What will prison do to my boy? I've heard about these prisons, Mr Forde; some of them are said to be training schools for terrorists. What chance has my boy got of surviving time in one o' them places? How do I know he won't come out more IRA than when he went in?'

'You're talking about Long Kesh,' I said. 'What they call the Provos' Sandhurst – but Tommy won't be going there; that's a top security prison.' I glanced at him. 'He'll probably go to Crumlin,' I said, hoping this would ease his mind. 'He'll meet terrorists in there, sure, but I believe that's where the strength of his home-life will come in. No one can say he *won't* get involved, but with a background of love in the home such as he's had I think there's every reason to believe he won't. Besides, if Tommy's decision to invite Christ into his life is genuine – and I believe it is, although time will tell – he'll have an inner strength that he knew nothing about before. And Mr Cummings and I will keep in touch with him.'

He leaned forward in his seat and peered at me through the dim light reflected from the headlamps.

'Will you really? That'd be such a help, Mr Forde.'

'Sure,' I said, 'we'll drop in to see him whenever we're down his way. But the biggest help will come from you and your family, and his friends – the right sort, of course. The more ties he has with home the stronger will be his defences. No, I don't think you need worry about Tommy. He's a good lad at heart.'

'Aye,' he said, biting his lip, 'he's a good lad ... '

He was silent for a while, but then said:

'I suppose you're a Protestant, Mr Forde?'

I hesitated, unsure of the reason for his question. A policeman can't help being suspicious. We were nearing the Falls Road and by this time Protestants with any sense wouldn't go near the place more often than they could help. But I judged that I was safe with this man.

'I am,' I said, 'although if you had put the question another way and asked me what religion I was I would have said I was a Christian.' I smiled at him. 'I've found that Christ isn't interested in labels, only people. But if I have to wear a label, yes, I'm a Protestant. Why do you ask?'

We were now in the Falls Road, one of Belfast's bleakest symbols of the great divide.

'It doesn't mean much, but I was going to say, I'm sorry.'

'Sorry?' I said. 'Sorry for what?'

'Sorry for what us Catholics are doin' to you.'

'We owe a few apologies ourselves,' I said. After a pause I added: 'Wouldn't it be something if we could get them all – everyone, Catholics, Protestants – to stretch out a hand and say sorry to one another.'

'Aye, it would,' he said flatly. 'The trouble is you'd never get 'em to agree who should be first!'

Several months later Tommy's case came up and he was sentenced to three years in prison. I told him that if he behaved himself he'd probably be out in two, with remission.

A few weeks passed by and a letter arrived on my desk at Donegall Pass. It read:

Dear Mr Forde,
My wife and me wanted to write to thank you for all the help you have given our Tommy. The sentence was a bit of a blow, but like you said he could be out sooner if he keeps his nose clean. We are very grateful for you and Mr Cummings putting in a good word to the judge. We saw Tommy again this morning and he is keeping well. My wife says to tell you that she has seen

a real change in him. Thanks once again. Our regards to your family.

God's blessing be with you.

Yours sincerely,

Archie Carson.

9

In self-defence

When I need peace like a gentle flowing river
I seek the source, the giver of life;
There my world-weary soul He will deliver
From the turmoil, the struggle and strife.

'Ben, it's here!'

Lily came smiling into the bathroom where I was shaving, a large flat parcel in her hand. She held it up for me to read the label which bore the name of the sender.

'The record! Oh, great stuff!'

'Shall I unwrap it while you finish in here?'

'Would you, love? We can have it on over breakfast.'

Minutes later Keri and Clive came bounding in with the record sleeve in their hands.

'Daddy, Daddy!' they chorused. 'Look!'

'It's you and Uncle David!' beamed Keri.

I turned and saw for the first time the photograph of David and myself holding our guitars and looking like a couple of Nashville hopefuls in our checked 'cowboy' shirts and deadpan expressions. At the top of the sleeve were the words: 'Fourteen Melodies of Praise'.

'Daddy, you're famous!' trilled Keri.

'Not yet I'm not,' I laughed. 'The record won't be on sale for another week or so. This is what you call an advance copy; one of the first ones.'

'Daddy, why aren't you smiling?' said Clive, looking hard at the sleeve.

'Well, because the man told me not to, I guess.'

'But didn't you have to say "cheese"? I thought you always have to say "cheese" when you have your picture taken.'

'Well, that's only to make you smile.'

'But you're not smiling,' Clive persisted.

Lily rescued me, calling out: 'Come on, you three, breakfast's on the table.'

'Come on,' I said, an arm round each of them, 'let's go and see what it sounds like.'

For all its shortcomings the record was well received across the land, and thanks to reviews and interviews in the press, local radio and Ulster Television, plus promotional opportunities through the RUC Choir and my singing engagements, the first pressing of two thousand copies was soon sold out and a second batch of one thousand rushed through to meet the steady demand.

At that time I already had a consistently busy diary of singing engagements, but as the record got around fresh interest was created and more and more invitations came in until I was booked over a year ahead with an average of two or three engagements each week. These took me to all manner of places, including coffee bars, hotels, old people's homes, borstals, factories, schools, town halls, and, of course, churches.

David shared a few of these engagements with me, as his own commitments would allow, but shortly after the record's release in September, 1975, a massive bomb demolished part of Castlereagh Police Station where David was based, and it brought to a head the anxieties he and his family had felt since returning to the Province from Australia. A few weeks after the explosion David hung up his uniform for the last time, and with it his hopes of building a life for himself and his family in his homeland. He had been back less than a year.

I didn't blame him. I doubt if any family moving to Belfast after years in a peaceful land would survive the pressures of life in 'Bomb City'. Since the beginning of this present terrorist campaign in 1968 it had been increasingly difficult to live an ordinary life here. You could never get away from the troubles, never forget the dangers. It was different for people like myself who had spent all their lives here. This was our home; we had walked its earth and breathed its air since before we could recall. It was our inheritance. And we loved it. We wouldn't give it up willingly, nor would we let it be snatched from us by force. And one day, perhaps a long way off, but one day peace would return like the dove and settle upon this battle-scarred land of ours, and in time the wounds would heal, and the bitterness fade away. Until that time we would smile and be brave and encourage one another and believe, like the psalmist, that although 'weeping may go on all night . . . in the morning there is joy'.

There must be few in this land of ours who have not wept as a result of the troubles, but rather than destroying the unity of our peoples, as the terrorists would like, the tears have strengthened us, drawn us closer together, and consequently I believe we are better people. The individual home may have suffered – and there are already too many empty places around our family tables – but the family of the people of Northern Ireland has flourished.

One of the evidences of this strengthening of the family spirit is the way in which people care for one another. Lily and I have experienced this in a very positive and moving way.

At a time when more and more policemen were being shot dead on their doorsteps or on their way to work, and it was obvious there would be no let-up in this critical situation, the folk living in our street and neighbouring streets came together at a public meeting in a local hall to discuss how they might help protect myself and other policemen living in the area. The answer, they felt, was to form a vigilante patrol with members taking turns to keep watch on our homes and, if necessary, actively defend them.

We were deeply touched by this expression of concern. After the critical attitude of many towards the RUC man during the propaganda campaign of 1974 this evidence of our neighbours' support and their willingness to put their own lives at risk in order to protect ours was most heartening. But we couldn't accept their offer. We police officers met to discuss the proposals and agreed that, grateful though we were, we could not allow others' lives to be endangered.

This sort of assistance was accepted in other parts of the Province, and I would be the last to speak a word against those colleagues who availed themselves of this form of protection, but I believed the vigilante patrol to be contrary to the spirit of the law.

Also, as a policeman I felt it was my responsibility to

accept whatever situations presented themselves and to deal with them as best I could. And certainly the policeman was better equipped to handle the terrorist than the teacher, the doctor, the garage owner and the many other members of the public who offered their services.

There was another reason why I could not go along with the vigilante patrol. In other areas I had seen this attitude and this involvement grow until it took on a more sinister face – the face of the illegal para-military organisations whose objectives are offensive rather than defensive. The acts of these bodies cannot be justified by their high-sounding principles. Whatever their motive for violence, whether it is so-called self-preservation, retaliation, retribution, or whatever, it cannot be excused. Murder is murder.

A common attitude in the Province is that it was necessary for the Protestants to form their own para-military groups in order to strike back at the Provisional IRA. The intention, it is said, was to deter the Republicans from attacking innocent citizens (and here the connection with the vigilante groups can be seen), but two wrongs never make a right and the tragic result has been further violence. This feud situation has escalated the number of casualties on both sides, and the RUC has been caught in the crossfire. In fact since the rise of the para-military organisations the policeman's life has been made doubly difficult because not only is he having to deal with the terrorist, but also with those who, seeking vengeance, have taken the law into their own hands. It is a vicious circle of death and the circle is widening all the time.

It was my concern that no more innocent, well-meaning groups should degenerate into yet more assassination squads that decided me against the vigilante patrol. Of the two choices, I think it preferable that policemen should occasionally know times of extreme danger and even feel unsafe in their own homes, than that they should accept protection from men who, having entered the fringe of lawlessness, may be enticed or dragged in further until they stand with blood on their hands.

It was about this time of the vigilante patrol that Neville, his wife Avril and their three children made one of their occasional visits for tea on Sunday afternoon. At the wives' insistence, Neville and I agreed not to talk shop, and we did very well through the lettuce and cold ham, but come the bread and jam and we had to hold our tongues. By the time the trifle arrived we couldn't help ourselves. Well, the subject of the safety of our homes was only half to do with work, so we thought we'd get away with it. As the conversation took its course we realised that Lily and Avril were just as ready to talk about this as we were. The children were happily occupied with cracking the latest jokes and testing the limits of their appetites, so we felt free to talk.

By now we had grown accustomed to taking various precautions around the home – annoying but necessary precautions such as having to scrutinise the post in case of letter bombs, checking the doorstep each morning for parcels or packets which may have contained explosives, and getting down and looking under the car before driving off. The greatest care had to be taken to identify unfamiliar callers to the house before removing the door-chain, and before retiring for the night a check had to be made on all the door and window locks which had been installed.

Some policemen went to even greater lengths, but we agreed that you had to draw the line at some of the security gadgets and systems available, otherwise the home became a prison, and though you may have been very safe in such a place you would also be pretty miserable. Instead of being a place to which you loved to return and where you were happy to spend time, it would be a constant reminder of the perils of your job and a place where you would be haunted by fear. That was not a home but a torture chamber.

After tea, when the children had gone out to play in the garden and we were attacking the washing-up, the question of self-protection and defence of the family came up. We all knew where we stood on this, but perhaps it encouraged us, especially the wives, to be reminded of how we would respond in a situation in which our lives or the lives of our loved ones were threatened.

'It used to worry me,' I said, 'whether as a Christian I would be willing to defend myself in a way that might harm another person, but when it happens, and it's you or him, you don't give it a second thought.'

Neville nodded his agreement. 'Did you hear about that case recently – that Christian girl who was threatened with rape?'

'Oh gosh, no!' said Lily. 'What happened, did she scream the place down?'

'No, apparently these two men forced their way into this home where there was a married couple and this girl. They decided to rape the wife in the presence of the

117

husband. Well, this girl took off upstairs and locked herself in her room. One of these fellas chased her and broke the door down, but by this time the girl had a gun in her hand. She fired and hit him in the leg, but he kept coming so she shot him dead.'

Avril shivered. 'Oh, how awful!'

'I couldn't do that,' said Lily. 'I'd probably drop dead with fright.'

'You may *think* you couldn't do it,' said Neville, 'but probably if you'd asked that girl beforehand if she could ever shoot someone she would have said no. But you can't answer that question because you just don't know until it happens.'

'Aye, that's it,' I agreed. 'All you can do is hope you're never faced with that choice, but if a man ever enters this house with a gun in his hand I know it's because he means to kill someone. And if I can't disarm him and my life is in danger of being ended then it's going to be either him or me.'

'Can we talk about something else?' said Lily. 'We don't want to depress ourselves with all this talk of guns.'

'Yes,' said Avril firmly. 'Tell us where you've been singing lately, Ben.'

That week God had given me opportunities to sing at a rally in Saintfield, a women's fellowship in Randalstown, and a working men's club on the outskirts of Belfast. Lily had already heard about these engagements, but she listened again as I told Avril how the Lord had used the occasions to bring an elderly lady to trust him for salvation, and how he challenged two men with the gospel at the working men's club. What I didn't tell her was that on the morning after I had been to that club a man's body was found in the doorway.

Occasionally there would be a lighter side to work; it was not all gloom and doom. We knew how to laugh, and sometimes we would find a source of amusement in the midst of the depressing details of the cases we were investigating.

One day I found myself questioning a young man about his membership of the IRA and his involvement in the hi-jacking of motor-vehicles. He was obviously a very nervous person and wanted to admit the part he had played in various crimes. He also co-operated in giving the names of other people involved in terrorist activities. From the RUC point of view he was most helpful.

When I had finished dealing with him I went back to Donegall Pass where I passed on certain details learned from this man which I thought would be of interest to Inspector George Bell, a uniformed Inspector with whom the CID worked quite closely.

'Did he give any other useful information?' the Inspector asked.

'Yes, there was one other thing,' I said, trying to keep a straight face. 'Tell me, where does your wife buy her sausages?'

He stared at me in disbelief for a moment, then the corners of his mouth turned up in a faint smile as he told me the name of his local butcher.

'Why do you want to know?' he asked.

'As long as she doesn't get them from –' and I said the name of a certain supermarket.

He was intrigued.

'What if she did?' he chuckled.

'Well, this fella works there as a butcher, and he says if you saw what went into their sausages you'd never eat another banger in your life!'

He roared with laughter and went off to share the joke with someone else.

On another occasion a man was brought in on a charge of aiding and abetting terrorists. He was a farmer and one of his outbuildings had been used for making and storing bombs. Not that he had given permission for this; typically, he had been told that the building was required for this purpose and that if he objected he would get trouble. And so the terrorists moved in.

One evening, when he was having difficulty getting his fire going in the kitchen, he started to look around in his outbuildings for something that would help the fire to catch. In the building used by the terrorists he came across a can of what he thought was paraffin.

'It seemed all right,' he told me, scratching his head. 'Smelt like paraffin, anyway. But when I poured a bit on the fire there was this almighty explosion. Knocked me across the room, it did – and blew the roof off!' He looked at me with a twinkle in his eye; he had a broad sense of humour. 'Still,' he chuckled, 'it got the fire goin'!'

Then there was the case of the terrorists who were planning to blow up a ship in Warrenpoint Harbour as a propaganda exercise. They decided a trial run would be in order, so off they went, complete with bomb and all the other equipment they thought they would need. Unfortunately their calculations failed to take into account the loading capacity of their vessel and they'd not gone fifty yards before the boat began to sink! The ducking didn't dampen their enthusiasm, however: they went ahead with their plans the following evening– and were promptly arrested by the marines!

Other situations would be comical if they weren't so tragic. One evening a young woman was brought in for questioning in relation to various terrorist activities. This woman had a wooden leg and during the interview she told me she had been approached by certain people who wanted her to carry incendiary bombs in the hollow part of this false limb.

'What did you say to that?' I asked.

She laughed shortly. 'I said, "No fear – if one o' them things goes off while I'm carryin' it I'll get me good leg full o' splinters".'

Tragic though it is to see such young people caught up in the hostilities which are ripping this land apart, those who suffer most in these families are not the guilty but the innocent: the parents. This is not to say that all parents are innocent. In this land there are mothers – and it's the mother who has the greatest influence over a child – who are so embittered that they train up their children to hate the people they consider their enemies. They even condone, if not encourage, violence, and I have heard a woman say of the murder of a British army officer, 'What does it matter – it was only a soldier.' It is the children of women like this who, by the time they are ten years old, are proficient in making small bombs, like the lethal 'nail bomb' in which six-inch nails are taped around a stick of dynamite.

But thank God these mothers are in the minority; most are decent people who have tried their utmost to keep their children from becoming involved, and it is they whose hearts are broken when their sons or even daughters are found to be mixed up in the killing or bombing.

Mary Cahill was such a mother. I met her in 1972 as a result of having to question two of her five sons. Life was not easy for this little woman – she had more than her fair share of domestic difficulties – but she was a genuine and warm-hearted person and I got on well with her. I had cause to meet her on a number of occasions, unfortunately owing to the various misdeeds of her sons, but through these meetings I was able to talk with Mary about God and what he could do for her and her family. When the record became available she expressed great interest and was most thankful for the copy I gave her. But as far as I was aware, despite our talks, Mary never made a personal commitment of her life to Christ. However, one evening I met her and she clasped my hands in hers. With eyes moist with tears she thanked me again for the record; but for that, she said, she would not be standing here now.

She readily explained: recently things had become so bad, the pressures so great, that she was on the verge of taking her life. In desperation, she had picked up 'Fourteen Melodies of Praise' and put it on the record player. As she listened she was struck by the words of hope in some of the songs, and as she thought of them, and as the music continued to flow, her attitude changed.

'Your record,' she said, 'saved my life.'

'No,' I said, 'God saved your life. He simply used the record to do it.'

I learned a lesson that night. The more I had listened

to the record the more concerned I had become that the quality of the production was not all that it could have been, although I believed it to be the best possible within the budget. Of course it is right that we should strive for the very best for our God, and there is absolutely no excuse for giving him our second best, but if the highest standards simply are not attainable, then God can and does use our efforts.

Through Mary, God showed me that he does not require us to be successful, only faithful. If we are faithful, he will do the rest.

10

Terror comes close

At times I feel my faith begin to waver,
When up ahead I see a chasm wide;
It's then I turn and look up to my Saviour,
I am strong when He is by my side.

As the cancer of violence spread throughout the body of
our land, so my field of operations widened. As the
terrorist moved farther afield to commit his outrage, so
the detective had to travel. Sometimes the distance meant
being away from home overnight, or if the inquiries
demanded it, a stay of two or three days would be
necessary.

One time I was down in Ballymena, County Antrim,
investigating the murder of a man who had been burned
to death during a series of bomb attacks on Ballymena's
shopping centre. On the last day I was there, bombs were
planted in another shopping area in Dunmurry, West
Belfast, where we had moved a few months earlier.
I heard about it when I got home that evening, for Lily
had been there; in fact she had been involved: the
terrorists had tried to hi-jack her car for their getaway.

The moment I stepped into the house I knew something was wrong. Lily looked shaken up; there wasn't
so much as a hint of her usual smile.

'Lily, are you all right?' I asked.

Tears that had been refused for hours now flowed freely as Lily rushed into my arms.

'Love, what's the matter?'

Clive came running from his room, his eyes wide with excitement.

'Dad, we were held up by some bad men and they tried to steal our car!' he gushed.

I stared at him for a moment while his words sank in.

'We had to go to the police station,' he went on, 'and there were bombs, Dad, and the man had a gun and –'

'Hang on, son,' I said, raising my hand. 'Let Mummy tell me.'

Lily stepped back and took a handkerchief to her eyes. She'd finished with the tears now.

'It's true,' she said, and gave a hearty blow into the handkerchief.

'Look, sit down,' I said, guiding her to the settee. 'Tell me all about it, from the beginning.'

'Well, I picked Clive up from school this afternoon as usual,' she began, regaining her composure, 'and there were a few things I wanted at the shopping centre so we drove in and I parked in the supermarket car park. I'd not even turned off the engine before a man opened the passenger door and got in beside me.'

Anger flared inside me, but I said nothing.

'I knew it was trouble, so I switched off and got out of the car. I don't know what I thought I would do. There was no one about and there was this other man standing there with his hand in his pocket, like as though he had a gun . . . ' She looked up at me, a trace of fear in her eyes. 'Oh, Ben, I was so frightened . . . '

I sat down beside her and took hold of her hand. 'Go on,' I said gently, hiding my anger. 'What happened next?'

'This other man got into the back seat with Clive and then he told me to get in; that I was to drive them.'

Clive was standing beside the settee, hopping from one foot to the other, bursting with excitement and reliving the event as Lily described it. To a six-year-old it was all a marvellous adventure. I smiled at him and he came and curled into my lap as Lily went on:

'I took the keys out of the ignition and said I wasn't doing anything till he let Clive out of the car, but he wouldn't, at first. So I just kept on at him to let Clive out and in the end he did. He had to get out himself to let Clive out, and then he snatched the keys and gave them to the other man who had moved across behind the wheel.' She looked at me, calmer now. 'Well, you know how many keys there are on my ring – door keys and church keys and all sorts – and he just couldn't find the right one. He kept saying, "Which key? Which key?", but I kept quiet. For a minute, though, I thought Clive was going to tell them – ' She looked at him fondly. ' – he started to point to the right one, but thank goodness I managed to signal to him to keep quiet. Then suddenly there seemed to be lots of people in the car park, and the men just gave up and ran off. Just after that we heard some bombs go off. They were over in the furniture warehouse. Then the police came . . . '

As Lily's voice trailed off, Keri came into the room and rushed over to greet me.

'Daddy,' she said softly, 'some bad men tried to take Mummy and Clive away in our car.'

126

'I know, sweetheart,' I smiled. 'And both Clive and Mummy were very brave, weren't they.' Then I turned to Lily and for the first time let my anger show as I said: 'You'd recognise them again, these men? 'Cause I'm going to get them, and when I do . . . '

I rolled Clive off my lap and got up to go to the hall.

'Ben, where are you going?' Lily asked anxiously. 'Don't do anything silly.'

'I'm going to make a phone call, that's all,' I said. 'Who did you speak to at the station? Who's on the case, do you know?'

'Ben, please – it's being taken care of,' Lily pleaded.

I picked up the phone and dialled the station. Under my breath I said, 'I'll take care of them all right if I get my hands on them.'

The anger did not last long. There was no point in harbouring hate or malice. It was not possible to confront these men who had threatened the safety of my loved ones. But had they been accessible at that time I realise I would have been tempted to sin. This is a natural reaction, of course; it is something that is in all of us. Looking back I thank God that my attempts to locate those men were unsuccessful and that therefore I wasn't faced with the temptation to wrong them.

This incident taught me two things. It reminded me very forcefully that I was still a sinner: that although by God's grace I had been saved from the wrath of his judgment, there was another sense in which I was still *being* saved, for I cannot be perfect this side of heaven. Not that this excuses my deliberate sin; as the apostle Paul writes: 'You can trust God to keep temptation from becoming so strong that you can't stand up against it . . . He will show you how to escape temptation's power.' That puts the onus squarely on my shoulders.

The other thing I learned was an insight into how the most loving and responsible people can act out of character and inflict harm or even commit murder. For when violence comes so close, perhaps maiming a loved one, or even taking their life, people can become eaten up with a hatred and bitterness that draws them into taking vengeance, and it is only after committing the deed that many realise how greatly they have acted against their moral principles.

From my own reaction that evening I could see how easy it would be for a man to let his feelings get the better of him. And this seemed to underline the need for every man to hand his life over to God, and to know his power within to resist sin. Even *with* Christ this is sometimes difficult, but always possible; without him all men will fail miserably.

As I thought on these things it was impressed upon me that, as a Christian, the key to resisting temptation and to loving my enemies is not found in reading the Bible, though it is through God's Word that we learn of his formula for success in these and other areas, but the key is found in prayer. If in the Bible we find instruction and direction for life's journey, in prayer we find the provision and the sustenance necessary for the course. Prayer is really feeding on God. Jesus said, 'I am the Bread of Life.' As we get to know him through talking to him, being quiet before him and allowing him to talk to us, so he feeds us with himself. There is no hunger of the human soul he cannot satisfy. And there is no need of the human heart he cannot meet. It is because he has met my own need, and abundantly blessed me beyond my hopes and desires, that I can confidently commend Jesus to all – the housewife, the policeman, the terrorist. But without prayer, that two-way, ever open channel of communication with God, this would be a different story.

That night, at the children's bedtime, we knelt as a family and thanked God for keeping us all safe that day, and then we asked that he would speak to those men who had planted those bombs and sought to take Lily's car. It was perhaps the most difficult prayer I had ever prayed, but it was also one of the most necessary.

'Lord,' I continued, 'let them come to know the love of Jesus through the cross.' And then I knew I had forgiven them. For the cross is the great leveller: there we all stand condemned; there we all find pardon.

The spirit of forgiveness is something Lily and I have sought to teach Keri and Clive throughout their childhood. One evening we had the satisfaction of realising that the message was getting through. I was kneeling beside Clive as he said his prayers before getting into bed. He was a little upset, having heard on the news that a policeman had been killed, and in his prayer he told God how he loved his Daddy, and that if they ever shot his Daddy (I awaited the next remark with great interest) he would like to be shot too, so that he could be with his Daddy. There was not so much as a hint of retaliation.

I know of only one way to bring to an end the centuries-long troubles in Northern Ireland. It is the way of the bended knee, the way of the forgiving spirit, the way of 'bring up a child in the way he should go, and when he is grown he will not depart from it'. This is where the battle must be won, in the home. The choice of war or peace is

9

in the hands of every parent in the land. As today's parents we may never see that peace, but by teaching them aright our children might one day inherit a land free of bitterness and strife. What greater gift could we leave them?

I suppose it was this same thought – this message of hope, this solution – which I was seeking to promote through the record. To my delight it was selling exceptionally well and it wasn't long before the record company was suggesting that a follow-up album should be made. They talked of a better quality of production, too. I explained about David having returned to Australia, but they seemed confident that a solo album would sell just as well, so we went ahead and made preparations for this. I wanted to include a lovely song called 'Jesus and Me', and as from the recording angle it *was* just Jesus and me we decided to use this as the title of the album.

This second record, released in autumn 1975, created fresh interest in 'the singing policeman'. The media obviously thought I was suitable interview material because 'Jesus and Me' resulted in a string of newspaper and magazine articles, all of which I welcomed as openings to witness for Christ and to share the gospel. However, these were also good opportunities to promote the record, which I was keen to do; obviously the more copies that were sold the more people would hear the gospel in song. But there was also a secondary reason why I wanted to see the albums being snapped up. It never occurred to me when I first thought of making a record that there were royalties to be had from each disc sold and monies on copies sold personally, and as the occasional cheque came through I realised that here was another way in which the records could work for the Lord. To date the receipts from those first two records have enabled me to donate more than £2,000 to various Christian charities. How grateful I am for that television programme which gave me the idea of the record; how thankful I have been for that Thursday night off.

There was to be a third record a year or so later, and its theme was to come out of another Thursday night; a night that was to bring black tragedy.

It was the 22nd January, 1976. As usual I had stayed home so that Lily could captain her Girls' Brigade. At twenty past nine the telephone rang and it was David Kernohan, my Sergeant.

In a voice that was shaky and unusually quiet, he said: 'Ben, there's been an accident, a terrible accident. It's Neville and Inspector Bell . . . there was an explosion . . . Oh God, they're both dead!'

'No, wait,' I said, 'there must be some mistake . . .'

11

The supreme sacrifice

These were His servants, in His steps they trod,
Following through death the martyr'd Son of God:
Victor He rose; victorious too shall rise
They who have drunk His cup of Sacrifice.

Just before seven o'clock that evening an anonymous telephone call had come through. There were guns stashed in a back yard in a house off the Donegall Road. Some officers went down to investigate and brought back a shotgun.

Neville was at his desk tending to some paperwork while his colleagues examined the gun. As they broke it open the action triggered explosives in the barrels. The blast killed two men. Inspector George Bell died from the force of the explosion. Neville Cummings lost his life after being struck by flying debris.

I replaced the telephone receiver, stunned. My best friend and a close colleague . . . Good men, full of faith, hope and charity, loving and loved . . . George and Neville – part of my life and work; as much a part of the daily routine as the air I breathed. But no more.

Bewildered, I paced through the silent house, going endlessly from room to room as though searching for something I knew I would not find, and all the while my mind tormented with fond picture-thoughts of these men. Especially Neville. How long had we worked together? How many years had we shared that desk, chatting, laughing, confiding, helping across it? Five years? Yes, but what years they were! Rich and full and overflowing with comradeship, friendship, fellowship... Why, Neville was more than part of my life – he was part of *me*! He couldn't die, he *couldn't*...

I was still dazed the next morning when I walked into Queen Street Police Station where I was working on a fraud case. I don't recall much of my activities that day, but the evening I remember well. The choir was booked to give a concert in a church hall and I took part as a matter of course. At the beginning we had a minute's silence while each man identified himself with the tragic loss the force had suffered in the past twenty-four hours. We have become used to this; it seems we have cause to mourn practically every time the choir performs. And mourn we do; there is a closeness, a oneness within the RUC which generates a very real sense of belonging and of caring for one another. It is a feeling which perhaps is not found in any other police force in the world. Not that it is something in which we would wish to boast; the circumstances which have brought it about are no cause for pride.

Of course, that night it was different for me; I had lost colleagues before, but never one so close as Neville. Indeed, there had never *been* another officer so close to me as Neville. We were pals, brothers in Christ, comrades in detection – everything which could weld two men together in an unwritten partnership. And now, in the deep silence of that minute's remembrance, all I could think was: It's over.

Looking back, I cannot remember feeling any bitterness or hatred towards those faceless men who did this thing. I had every reason to hate. But all I recall is an embracing sense of peace. God's peace. It is a remarkable phenomenon, a touch of what it must be like in God's presence; the undisturbedness of which Jesus spoke when he said: 'Peace I leave with you. My peace I give unto you. And the peace I give isn't fragile like the peace the world gives.' When you experience it you know it is just as he said it would be.

The following Saturday I went with many other police colleagues to the funeral of Inspector George Bell at the Church of Ireland in the Lisburn Road. George had been a much loved member of this church and it was packed to the doors. Truly he would be sorely missed, not only by his family but also here by his friends as well as at Donegall Pass by his colleagues. Yet out of the tears and tragedy of that occasion was to come a message of triumph. It was here that for the first time I heard and sang a hymn entitled 'The Supreme Sacrifice'. Its message, of course, refers to Christ's supreme sacrifice for sinners on the cross, and it brought to mind that verse from John's Gospel: 'No greater love hath any man than this, that he lay down his life for his friends.' But clearly this hymn had relevance to the death of my colleagues also, for without doubt they had lost their lives for their friends.

So moving were the words of this hymn, and so stirring

the melody, that as we sang I could almost touch the sense of comfort, of optimism and of consolation which was nurtured within our hearts and then released through our lips to fill that echoing building.

The heaviness of heart was still there, the sorrow of our loss still prompted tears, but in the midst of the darkness there was an inner light. And it seemed that the more cruelly the darkness pressed in on it, the brighter the light shone.

It was then I knew that I must record 'The Supreme Sacrifice'. Its message was too big to confine within church walls.

On Sunday I went to Newtownbreda Baptist Church for Neville's funeral service. From where I sat I could look across and see Avril and the three children. They were all so very brave that day, although not surprisingly Avril looked weak and hunched in her green tweed coat. At one point she turned and looked at me, unseeing, her face white beneath her dark hat, and her eyes hollow with silent suffering. And once, as the coffin was carried in, I glanced across at her and wondered if she would be able to bear the pain. Moisture was clouding my eyes now, and as I looked, the light from the window played a trick through the tears and made it appear as though there was a soft glow behind Avril, right up close to her back. It was just a trick, an illusion. Either that or there was an angel with his arms round Avril, holding her up.

I couldn't go to the graveside. Towards the end of the service the shock I had felt on Thursday evening began to wear off, and in its place came thundering waves of grief. The love I felt for my friend and the loss which crowded into my mind spread through my being like a bursting, empty ache, and I broke down, overwhelmed, upon my chair.

When the service was over I was helped to my car – I declined the offers to drive me – and then I was away home, peering through water-filled eyes as I travelled the seemingly endless two or three miles to Dunmurry.

There, blinded by tears, I fell on to the settee and wept myself dry.

I cried for three hours.

Oh, Neville . . .

Those who know Belfast are used to seeing a sign hanging in various shops, pubs and hotels only a day or so after the premises have been partly destroyed by bombs. The sign says: 'Business As Usual.' On the morning after this the most traumatic day in my life I had to hang that sign on my heart and go out and carry on with the job. It wasn't easy, and yet it wasn't difficult. The previous evening I had thrown myself upon the Lord, crying, 'Why? Why?' I did not blame God, nor have I since, for I know that sin, not God, killed Neville. But 'Why?' No answer came, and yet God did reply with the comfort of his Holy Spirit and the assurance and strength of his Word. Several verses came to me: 'Thou wilt keep him in perfect peace whose mind is stayed on Thee'; 'The Lord is at my right hand'; 'Blessed are they that mourn, for they shall be comforted.'

As I left the house that morning – the morning I was to return to Donegall Pass – I turned to Lily and another scripture came to me.

'Don't worry,' I said, 'they can kill the body, but they can't kill the soul.'

At the station I learned that the explosion had punched out the windows of the office and ripped a desk and some chairs apart. But the debris was long gone; as I'd expected, the office had been cleaned up, the walls repainted and the windows reglazed the day after the incident. Morale must be maintained – policemen are only human beings; they cannot be expected to pursue their duty amidst the litter of death.

In the doorway of the office I stopped and looked around. Our desk – my desk now – stood unscathed, and yet utterly broken. On one corner the typewriter stood mute and brave, its casing dented when it had been flicked off the desk and dashed against the wall as effortlessly as though it were a paper cup. The blast had blown its keys up into a bunch of metal fingers, like hands in front of a face. Between the rollers stood an unfinished report. But Neville was so meticulous, so methodical, I told myself – and for one blind moment that morning I turned quickly towards the door, thinking I had heard his cheery laugh in the cold corridor outside and expecting him at any second to breeze in, his eyes laughing, his lips smiling, to make that old machine rattle and ring expertly once more.

Later that morning a telephone call came through for Neville.

'He's not here at the moment,' I said automatically, and then: 'I mean, he's . . . ' And the rest of the words wouldn't come, as though they had screwed themselves up into a lump as big and hard as a billiard ball and jammed in my throat.

137

As the weeks wore on I began gathering material for a third album which I felt should be titled 'The Supreme Sacrifice' and have the message of that hymn as its theme. It was to be an album of promise, of hope and of victory. But it wouldn't be recorded by Outlet. As a result of 'Jesus and Me' I had received an invitation to record with a London based company, Pilgrim Records, which specialised in Christian music. I made the move reluctantly, for I had much to be thankful to Outlet for, and I remain grateful to them for all they did in helping me to establish my recording ministry (I am pleased to say that I am still on excellent terms with William McBurny and his colleagues at Outlet), but we must ever be open to opportunities to make headway in our service for the Lord, and it was clear that, with many years' experience of recording gospel music, and with extensive technical facilities at their disposal, Pilgrim had much to offer the Christian artist. Also, their distribution network covered a far wider field than was available before. Naturally these things appealed, but in addition there was a concern for the spiritual content and quality of the material to be recorded; a desire to see the records they produced being used to minister to the listener. All these advantages, plus the fact that Lily and I felt right before God about making the changeover, led me to sign with Pilgrim. And it wasn't long before positive plans were being laid for 'The Supreme Sacrifice'.

But there appeared to be a problem. Each time I tried to rehearse this song at home I found I could not get through it; I would get so far and then, overcome by the memories this song evoked and by the powerful message it contained, I would find my voice failing me, my control snatched away by the emotions welling up inside me.

Came the day of the recording at studios in Eastbourne, Sussex, and I still hadn't managed to sing the title hymn right through. What was I to do? I felt convinced God would have me record this song – indeed, it was the crux of the album; something I believed God had implanted in me as a vision – but I seemed unable to cope with it. As Lily and I had travelled over to London on the plane, along with Roxaline and Artie Bowman whom the company had agreed to include in the backing musicians, I had told myself it would be all right in the studio. But it wasn't. Each time I did the 'ghost' singing of 'The Supreme Sacrifice' to enable the musicians to record the backing (this is recorded separately from the vocals) I found I still couldn't finish the song. That wasn't so bad, but when it came to actually taping the vocals and I couldn't do any better the technicians began to get concerned. Studio time is expensive and of course there was a limit to the time allocated for the recording. Understandably, after a couple of unsuccessful 'takes' the producer said, 'Let's drop this one and use another.'

'No,' I said, 'it's got to go on. We'll try it again – it'll be all right this time.'

And it was. I sent up an SOS prayer and down came the answer. Today this album stands as a testimony not only to Christ's supreme sacrifice and to the selfless dedication of my RUC colleagues who have laid down their lives for their friends, but also as a testimony to God's provision in the hour of need. Without his direct undertaking 'The Supreme Sacrifice' would not have been recorded that day, or perhaps since. Not that God made it easy for me to get through the song; the Bible tells us that 'his grace is sufficient', and that is what he gave me – his sufficiency. No more. But absolutely no less. When the hymn was finished God gave me the release I needed from the tensions which had built up inside me each time I had tried and failed to practise it: I sat down and wept. Wept for Neville, for Inspector Bell, for all my colleagues who had perished under the proud but battered banner of the RUC . . .

It's good to be able to weep. Some men might say it is unmanly and perhaps would resist tears they might otherwise shed, but theirs is the loss if they never learn to cry. God is not ashamed of our tears, and I believe that if our weeping is done openly before the Lord then he takes it and uses it for blessing. The psalmist says that God 'stores my tears in a bottle', and again, 'He who sows in tears shall reap with joy'.

Looking back across the few short years which have passed since the tragic deaths which inspired 'The Supreme Sacrifice', God has indeed shown me the truth of this promise. Yes, we have wept, but we have also had the joy of seeing people in this land turning to Christ for forgiveness and salvation as a direct result of this recording. Others have found comfort and peace and the strength to carry on after losing loved ones at the hand of the terrorist. All this is no thanks to me or anyone else involved in the making of the record. It is simply the grace of God. In his love he has taken up our efforts and touched them with his Spirit so that they might bring blessing to man and glory to himself. And in his faithfulness he has not let the deaths of these dear men go to waste. For he has honoured their willingness to lay down their lives for the good people of this land, and with their blood he has watered and nourished seeds of hope and faith and victory sown here and there as the Spirit wills.

12

A hard road to travel

Thy way, not mine, O Lord,
However dark it be:
Oh, lead me by thine own right hand,
Choose thou the path for me.

Not so long ago I called round to see Avril one afternoon.
A few days earlier, speaking on the telephone to Lily, she
had asked if we could get her some cooking apples from
our friend's orchards near Portadown the next time we
were over that way. Lily got her a boxful and I put them
in the boot of the car so that I could drop them in when
I was next passing.

She must have seen me coming up the garden path
because the front door opened before I reached it.

'Your apples, Avril,' I smiled.

Her eyes lit up. 'Oh, thanks, Ben. How much do I owe
you? Could you put them in the garage – then come in
for a cup of tea. We could sit in the garden. It's nice now.'

While she was making the tea I stood in the hall and
looked around at Neville's handiwork. I had seen it all
before many times, but it never failed to impress me. He
had done a lot to this house, transforming it into a very
comfortable and convenient home. When Andrew, their
third child, had come along unexpectedly Neville had

built an extra bedroom in the roofspace; and downstairs he had put in a second toilet without so much as a thought for a plumber. He was good at that sort of thing.

Avril read my thoughts and as she came out of the kitchen with a tray of tea things in her hands she stopped for a moment and joined me in looking around.

She said softly: 'Neville loved this place.'

I nodded slowly. 'He made a grand home for you all. Better job than I could have made. I don't know how he did it, where he found the time.'

She smiled gently, remembering. 'He used to work away furiously,' she said, 'as though there wasn't a minute to spare.' And then she paused, realising what she had said. But bravely she went on: 'I used to say to him, "What's the hurry?", and he would say, "I want it finished for you . . . " ' She paused again, blinking back a tear, and then said, more brightly: 'It was a means of relaxation for him; a complete change from his work.'

Avril led the way out through the back of the house to a couple of garden chairs beside the rose bed. It was pleasant there in that little narrow strip of garden with a lilac bush sheltering us from the slight breeze and the sun playing its gentle heat and soft light upon us. So pleasant, in fact, that we might not have been in Belfast at all, so remote did we seem from the troubles. And yet it was because we were in Belfast that I was here.

As Avril poured the tea I was cheered by the fact that she had spoken so freely of Neville. Over the past three years Lily and I had visited her many times, but never before had she been able to bring herself to talk of him as she had done this afternoon. But I soon discovered that she wanted to talk, and that it was as much for her own benefit as mine. Those three years must have been like a long, cruel winter to her; perhaps this was her spring.

She passed me a cup of tea and then looked up at the back of the house.

'We've been here getting on for six years now. Doesn't seem like it.'

'*Tempus fugit*,' I remarked, not knowing quite what to say.

There was a long silence, and at last she said:

'He used to work so hard at everything. I used to say it was ridiculous to get up early in the morning and work till the small hours of the next day, him coming home looking drained, his face grey. But he always said it had to be done; that his boss wasn't man but God, and that he had to answer to him, whether he did his job well or not . . . '

I thought it wouldn't hurt to pursue this line of thought, so long as I was careful what I said. A wound such as she had suffered does not heal quickly; even after three years it would still be very tender.

I said: 'Aye, no one did his job better than Neville.' And then, because it seemed the right thing to say, and because I wanted to say it, I went on: 'I can't tell you how much we miss him, Avril. I think of him every day . . . '

She looked at me and smiled, but there was sadness in her eyes. There was another long pause while we sipped the tea. Then, slipping into a reverie, as though to protect herself from her own words, she spoke her thoughts. Beginning slowly, she said:

'He came home that night for his tea and then helped me with the dishes. Then he kissed me goodbye and took

Sharon to her music lesson on the way back to work. That was the last time I saw him . . .

'That night I was cutting out a dressing gown for Sharon on the living room floor and there was a knock at the door. It was a sergeant and a woman officer; they said there'd been an accident.

'I had to get one of the neighbours to stay with the boys and explain where Sharon was so that she could be brought home. Then I got into the police car to go to the hospital. Every traffic light was red and I thought the journey would never end. And while I wondered how badly Neville was injured a voice spoke to me so plainly: "The Lord gave, the Lord hath taken away. Blessed be the name of the Lord." ' She paused. 'At last we reached the hospital and I was taken into a small room, where a nurse asked me what seemed irrelevant questions. Then a young doctor came in and asked me if I was Mrs Cummings. When I said I was, he said: "I'm sorry, but your husband is dead." '

She began to shake a little so that I had to take the cup and saucer from her hand.

'We'll talk about something else,' I said, but I don't think she heard me. She wanted to go on. Perhaps she had to.

'I couldn't take it in. The nurse said they couldn't do anything for him. I remember her giving me tea to drink and then two nurses took me to see Neville.

'I said, "He's just sleeping." But the nurse told me to have a good cry, and I thought, "How can I cry when all I want to do is to lie down and die beside my beloved Neville." My heart was like a stone in my breast and remained like that for months . . . '

A minute passed before she went on: 'When they brought me home, our pastor, Pastor Fenton, was waiting and he came in with me while I told Peter and Sharon that their Daddy was with the Lord; that he had taken their Daddy home to be with him.

'My sister came up as soon as she heard and my parents came in the early hours of the morning. Neville's family came up the next morning.

'The next day Andrew told me that he wanted to die too because he wanted to be with his Daddy. Later on, he said his Daddy was upstairs, and when I tried to find the right words to explain to him, he said, "Yes, Daddy is upstairs in heaven." '

The darkest part over, she emerged from the reverie, her thoughts returning to the sunlit garden. Looking up at me, she said: 'People ask me how I ever got through the funeral, but you know, the presence of the Lord was all around me and it was a living presence, cushioning me from everyone and everything and carrying me through minute by minute. The Lord was with me in it all and upheld me.'

For a fleeting moment my mind went back to that service and I thought of the angel and wondered.

Avril refilled my cup as she went on: 'Those first months were awful ... All I could think was, "Why? Why?" – and I had this urge to be doing something all the time. I couldn't eat; in fact I lost two stone practically overnight. Everyone urged me to eat and keep my strength up for the children's sake, but how can you eat when everything tastes like cardboard?

'I had to start driving again and Sergeant Kernohan and Pastor Fenton went with me to give me confidence;

I trembled so much. People told me to have a good cry, but, you know, I couldn't do this until almost a year had passed.'

I looked at her in enquiry; that's a long time to hold back the tears.

'Yes,' she said, 'I'd gone for a routine cancer test and when a week or so later I received a letter asking me to go for another one, I thought I must have the disease. This was just too much . . . I took the letter and wept to the Lord about it and about the children being left without father or mother. I wept away all the tears that should have been wept over the months since Neville had . . . '
She paused, then brightened visibly. 'The Lord heard my prayer; the test was clear. I'd been sent the second appointment because of a clerical error.'

I smiled. 'The Lord's way,' I said. 'He knew you needed a good cry.'

She nodded, and looked away down the garden. 'The worst part now is knowing that I'm only half of myself; half of the one we were. It's been so hard, coping on my own, even with the everyday things. Making decisions is still difficult, but I seem to do things automatically. I still can't cope with the unexpected, though. I tremble all over if I have to do something I've not prepared myself for . . .

'I know many widows resort to drink or pills, and I suppose I could have gone the same way if it hadn't been for the Lord. Without him I don't think I could have come this far. Sometimes the hurt is almost impossible to bear . . .

'Someone said it takes three or four years to get over it, but I can't see that now. Pastor Fenton says perhaps you never get over it, but in time you learn to live with it. I think probably he's right, so I don't look too far ahead but just live a day at a time. With the Lord's strength I've found I can do that, and sometimes I find there aren't enough hours in the day.' She turned to me and smiled. 'Perhaps I try to do too much, but I find it best to keep myself occupied, rather than give myself time to think.'

There was a noise at the side of the house and the gate opened. It was Peter, Avril's eldest at seventeen, and the spitting image of Neville. He didn't see us at first and Avril called out to him. He came smiling down the garden path, his tie undone and his football gear sticking out of his school bag.

'Hello, Peter,' I called. 'Football today? Good game?'

He smiled in recognition, then screwed up his face. 'Rotten game,' he said with feeling. 'Lost three one.'

'You'll have to change your goal-keeper,' I laughed. 'Was he half asleep?'

'Too fat!' he grunted. 'Can't bloomin' well move!'

I laughed again, and Peter turned to his mother. 'Any iced drinks, Mum?'

'In the fridge. I got some this morning. But save some for Sharon and Andrew. I know what a guzzler you are!'

'I'm a growing lad!' he protested, and walked back up the path, breaking off in mid-stride to aim a kick at a stray dog-daisy hanging over the path.

When he was out of earshot I said: 'He's a growing lad, all right. Walks and talks just like his Dad, too.' It was harmless to say such a thing now; perhaps it was even helpful. Avril watched her son disappear into the house and smiled fondly.

'Where are the others?' I asked.

Avril glanced at her watch. 'Sharon's having tea with a friend and Andrew's still at school; his music lesson.' Then there was a long silence, broken only by a clinking of glasses and Peter whistling intermittently in the kitchen. At last Avril said: 'I'm glad I have them; I know I have to keep on for their sakes. But I know I can't be father *and* mother to them and they miss Neville so much. Sometimes my heart is so sore for them, but they seem to have adapted and they help me over the difficult days with their chat about school and so on. And I'm so thankful that they all love the Lord; I think we're closer because of that . . . '

I nodded, understanding fully. 'You can't go wrong if you keep close to him.'

She smiled. 'He's been so faithful. You know, we've always had enough for our everyday needs, and to spare. And I've become so assured of his love and care for us day by day that, although I still don't understand it, I'm aware that he did know best; he does do all things well.' She fought back a sudden watering of the eyes and went on: 'I know that he has taken Neville home to be in his safe keeping and that the children and I will one day be re-united with him.'

She threw back her head, blinking away the tears, and for a moment in that soft sunlight she seemed quite radiant.

'It's a hard road to travel,' she said, 'but when you reach this point you find that your heavenly Father undertakes in everything . . . '

As we stood at the gate a little while later, Avril said: 'Forgive me for going on so, Ben. I'm sure you didn't

come here just to listen to me pouring my heart out . . .
But thanks, anyway; thanks for listening.'

'Thanks for telling me,' I said. 'It's probably done us
both good.'

'I hope so,' she said, almost apologetically.

'Sure it has,' I said, and wondered whether I should
tell her what had been on my mind for some time. Well,
now was as good a time as any.

'I think we can all learn from one another's experi-
ences. I think even the man in the street, the people we
don't even know, can get something out of what we've
been through.'

She looked at me expectantly, knowing I was working
up to something.

'Like you said, Avril, it's a hard road to travel. I
haven't been through the grief – well, not like you have –
but I've known some tough times in this land of ours and
maybe there are people out there who might be helped
in their troubles if they knew how we've fared in our
own.' I hesitated. 'What would you think,' I said, 'if I
told you I was considering writing it all down in a book?'

Postscript

These closing pages are being written during a week in which all police leave in Northern Ireland has been cancelled because the terrorists are celebrating the eighth anniversary of the introduction of internment (which, incidentally, was brought to an end in December, 1975). When terrorists celebrate they don't take a holiday – they step up the killings and bombings. So far this week five men have died. I have been involved in the murder investigations of three of these men . . .

On Monday, at about ten o'clock in the morning, the telephone rings with an urgent request for assistance. A plain-clothed policeman, sitting in an unmarked car outside a courthouse in Armagh, has been murdered. Another car – a red Ford – moved slowly past the officer's vehicle and its occupants opened fire with high-powered weapons. These arms are capable of killing at a range of two miles or more, so someone shot from several feet stands no chance. The victim, a middle-aged constable, died instantly. Claiming responsibility for this act is the INLA (Irish National Liberation Army), a recently formed terrorist organisation which made its murderous debut with the assassination of Mr Airey Neave at Westminster in March of this year.

As soon as the phone is slammed down, four members of our unit are selected and sent speeding the thirty-eight miles to the scene of the crime. I'm one of them.

Another murder investigation is underway, in what is now regarded as 'bandit country'. Close to the County Monaghan/Armagh border, and consisting mainly of dense countryside, this is an area in which there is a great deal of terrorist activity. Police and army manoeuvres in this part of Ulster are accompanied by very high risks and only a fool doesn't keep looking over his shoulder.

On the Thursday morning a car suspected of being the one used by the assassins is reported abandoned and burnt out on the Armagh/Benburb Road.

Three of us drive out to inspect this vehicle, aware that even this could be a trap to lure yet more members of the security forces to their deaths. Members of the UDR and Police Reserves are already at the scene and as we get out of our car we glance furtively around at the hedgerows and woods surrounding us, our hands never far from our guns.

Our inspection of the vehicle over, we return to the police station in Armagh and add the information we have just gleaned to what we already know. Slowly the picture begins to take shape – but like a jig-saw only just begun there are many pieces to fit in place before the perpetrators of this murder will be facing charges.

As we sit around the table discussing what line of inquiry to pursue, suddenly Armagh's tranquil air is split by the most horrific crash: somewhere not too far away a massive bomb has just gone up. We know it is a big one because the windows rattle violently and we feel the vibrations from the distant wrenching of the earth in the very floor beneath our feet.

Within minutes the location of the explosion has been pin-pointed: a culvert about three miles outside Armagh on the Benburb Road, close to where we inspected the abandoned car.

The colour drains from our faces and nausea grips our stomachs as we realise that we drove over that culvert not twenty minutes ago.

We pile into the car and race to the scene, knowing full well that once more we may be going like lambs to the slaughter: the element of surprise is always on the terrorist's side. The car screeches to a halt and we spill out on to a sickening scene over which the dust has yet to settle. The evidence speaks for itself. The culvert has gone, its stones hurled five hundred yards in all directions. In its place stands a vast crater fourteen feet deep. To either side trees lie on their sides, uprooted. With its nose buried in the shallow stream which flows beneath the culvert lies a mangled army patrol van. A few yards down the road stands the escorting vehicle. This has come under fire from machine-guns. The soldiers in this vehicle escaped death. The two men in the blown-up patrol van were not so fortunate. The bomb, a landmine detonated from a hillside overlooking this stretch of road, was a huge one – 500 lbs. No one could survive the blast created by that amount of explosives.

One of the dead men was nineteen, the other twenty. They had been serving in Ulster exactly one week.

Horrified and sickened by the bloody mess, their colleagues drag the bodies from the wreckage. An army doctor – a young woman, her face pale – steps in and quickly does what is necessary before pronouncing the men dead.

One of my colleagues throws his hands in the air, curses, and cries that if there's a God at all up there why does he allow this?

Garry Craig, a Christian colleague, replies softly that it's true God allows it but he doesn't condone it; that God has given man a free will and the choice is his.

I move to the edge of the crater and stand looking down into the stream, now running dark with oil and dirt. A lone eel, encountering the pollution, wriggles furiously to one side, only to find itself being dragged into the mud. For a moment my thoughts turn to the callous murderers who, unless they find Christ, will one day squirm before the judgment and wrath of God. And on that day there will be no escape; as the apostle Paul writes, 'You can't fool God; every man will reap what he has sown.'

An army helicopter comes whirring noisily over the hill, snatching my thoughts back to the frustration and futility of the deaths of these two men, the breath of life blasted out of their young bodies at the press of a button.

This is the enemy we are dealing with daily in Northern Ireland. His methods are sophisticated and ruthless. He knows no honour and holds but one principle: the end justifies the means. But as I fight on in my work – and out of twenty years of police duty I have been fighting for fifteen and a half; I have known only four and a half years of normality – I have to ask whether *any* end could justify the terrible damage caused to people and property which I encounter day by day.

Perhaps, though, the greater tragedy is the damage which the perpetrators of these crimes do to themselves – for bitterness and hatred are as lethal as any bomb, if not more so – for bombs destroy only the body; bitterness and hatred will destroy the soul. Certainly the hard-line terrorist does not fear for his life, otherwise he would not be able to engage in murder, but does he not fear for his soul? Life, after all, doesn't go on for very long – seventy years if we are fortunate – but God's Word tells us clearly that after death comes the Judgment and then we shall realise we are in eternity where each of us will receive his just rewards. Principles, nationalities, denominations will count for nothing in that day. The soul in eternal anguish will derive no comfort from the belief that the deeds which brought him or her into end-less damnation were all in a good cause. The border between North and South will mean nothing then. Can it be worth the bloodshed – and the self-destruction – now?

Until such time as the terrorist sees these issues in their true perspective, however – or until a peaceful settlement is reached – I fear that the killing will go on. And members of the Royal Ulster Constabulary will continue to be amongst the assassins' targets.

But we shall not be frightened off. With every new tragedy – and to date more than 3,500 of my colleagues have been injured, some of them more than once, and over 120 murdered – the force wipes away its tears, grits its teeth, and digs its heels in a little more.

Statistically, every RUC man stands at least a fifty-fifty chance of being hit, and that's not a comforting thought to go to bed with. Yet we battle on, each man hoping he won't be next, but knowing there's every chance he might be.

It is no exaggeration to say that the bravery of the men and women who have chosen to do this dangerous job is, by any standard, outstanding. Their loyalty, too, is remarkable. More than a dozen men who have lost arms, legs or eyes during the present troubles are back on duty with the RUC. Perhaps the supreme example of courage and dedication is the officer (he modestly prefers to remain anonymous) who, after seven months in hospital following a booby-trap explosion, returned to duty with a metal leg, a false eye and an artificial arm. Surgeons did not expect him to live.

Blown up in the same incident was another officer. Regardless of multiple serious injuries he crawled three quarters of a mile to get help.

No wonder the RUC has won more gallantry awards than any other force in the world.

Yet we would shy away from the word 'hero'. The media might care to call us such, and Her Majesty may graciously pin medals to our tunics, but when all is said and done even the most decorated man would shrug his shoulders and protest that he was only doing his job – even though he may have acted far, far beyond the call of duty.

But there *are* heroes in this crucified land of ours. You

won't find them down by the railway embankment on a bitter night, their battledress frozen to the earth; you won't find them walking into a beating in the Falls Road; you won't find them searching for a bomb in Botanic avenue; you won't even find them in uniform or in any other way on the RUC payroll. More than likely you'll find them at the kitchen sink, fighting back the tears, asking God for the umpteenth time 'Why?', determined not to give way to the same bitter thoughts which took the dearest person on earth from them, and getting the kids off to school because you just can't give up.

It's there in the home, around the table where the family circle is now for ever broken, that you'll find the real heroism of Northern Ireland. It is the heroism that says no to defeat, grasps shakily at the belief that somehow the sacrifice must be worthwhile, and dares to believe that peace will come.

Peace. It is the sweet dream we must pursue. But is it no more than a dream?

When I consider how long this present terrorist campaign has gone on, how relentlessly it is pursued, how increasingly sophisticated the tactics and weapons that are used, I question whether a political settlement is possible at this time. Naturally, each fresh peace initiative is welcomed and viewed with hope, but at the time of writing I regret that I don't feel enthusiastic about a constitutional solution.

I'm not saying peace is impossible. It *is* possible. But, as I have sought to indicate throughout the chapters of this book, we must look to God's solution, not man's. I would suggest that man's way looks at the trouble within the nation and works back to the peace of the individual, while God's way looks at the trouble within the individual and works forward to the peace of the nation.

I believe – no, I *know* – God's solution will work. I am utterly confident because I am conscious of his victory in my own life and in the lives of others. But to gain that victory we need help, and as I stood by that bomb crater in Armagh and looked away to the slope from which the explosives were detonated, my eyes were drawn upwards to the top of that hill and I was reminded of the only one who can give that help, as into my mind came the words of a song by Marijohn Wilkin. Entitled 'The Mighty Hills of God', it's based on Psalm 121, which begins: 'I will lift up mine eyes unto the hills, from whence cometh my help. My help cometh from the Lord, who made heaven and earth.'

It was not the first time I had found myself considering the lyrics of a gospel song at the scene of a murder, for music has meant so much to me in my fight against crime, and in particular my fight against many terrorist type acts. Especially has it been a source of great strength to me in combating the effects of these things on my life.

Driving the weary miles home that night, the ugly details of the day's work still vivid in my thoughts, my mind turned to another song:

Peace, perfect peace, death shadowing us and ours,
Jesus has vanquished death and all its powers.

Jesus. He's the answer. And as I turned off the motor-

158

way once more and headed down into the angry valley which is Belfast I thought of him:

My life amongst death.
My light amidst darkness.
My hope in 'Bomb City'.